AAT

DEVOLVED ASSESSMENT KIT

Foundation Unit 2

Making and recording payments

August 2000 first edition

This new Devolved Assessment Kit follows the revised Foundation Standards of Competence. It contains:

- The **revised Standards in full**, including guidance from the AAT on **evidence requirements and assessment strategy**

- **Practice activities** to bring you up to speed on certain areas of the Standards

- **Trial Run Devolved Assessments**

All activities and assessments have full solutions included in this Kit.

FOR 2000 AND 2001 DEVOLVED ASSESSMENTS

BPP Publishing
August 2000

First edition August 2000

ISBN 0 7517 6231 8

British Library Cataloguing-in-Publication Data
*A catalogue record for this book
is available from the British Library*

Published by

*BPP Publishing Limited
Aldine House, Aldine Place
London W12 8AW*

www.bpp.com

*Printed in Great Britain by W M Print
45 –47 Frederick Street
Walsall
West Midlands WS2 9NE*

All our rights reserved. No part of this publication may be reproduced, stored in a retrieval system or transmitted, in any form or by any means, electronic, mechanical, photocopying, recording or otherwise, without the prior written permission of BPP Publishing Limited.

©

*BPP Publishing Limited
2000*

Contents

Page

INTRODUCTION (v)

How to use this Devolved Assessment Kit – Unit 2 Standards of Competence - Assessment strategy

		Questions	*Answers*

PRACTICE DEVOLVED ASSESSMENTS

1	Powell Cars	3	171
2	Ives	15	179
3	Conway	53	201
4	Micawber	63	205
5	Needham Baddely	69	209

TRIAL RUN DEVOLVED ASSESSMENTS

1	Barkers	89	217
2	Best-Books	115	231
3	Grow-Easy	125	237
4	Workbase Office Supplies	137	243
5	Paper Products	149	247
6	Catering Contracts	159	251

ORDER FORM

REVIEW FORM & FREE PRIZE DRAW

HOW TO USE THIS DEVOLVED ASSESSMENT KIT

Aims of this Devolved Assessment Kit

> To provide the knowledge and practice to help you succeed in the devolved assessment for Foundation Unit 2 *Making and Recording Payments*.

To pass the devolved assessment you need a thorough understanding in all areas covered by the standards of competence.

> To tie in with the other components of the BPP Effective Study Package to ensure you have the best possible chance of success.

Interactive Text
This covers all you need to know for devolved assessment for Unit 2. Icons clearly mark key areas of the text. Numerous activities throughout the text help you practise what you have just learnt.

Devolved Assessment Kit
When you have understood and practised the material in the Interactive Text, you will have the knowledge and experience to tackle this Devolved Assessment Kit for Unit 2. This aims to get you through the devolved assessment, whether in the form of a simulation or workplace assessment.

Recommended approach to this Devolved Assessment Kit

(a) To achieve competence in all units you need to be able to do **everything** specified by the standards. Study the Interactive Text very carefully and do not skip any of it.

(b) Learning is an **active** process. Do **all** the activities as you work through the Interactive Text so you can be sure you really understand what you have read.

(c) After you have covered the material in the Interactive Text, work through this **Devolved Assessment Kit**.

(d) Attempt the **Practice Devolved Assessments**. They are designed to test your competence in certain key areas of the Standards of Competence, but are not as comprehensive as the ones set by the AAT. They are a 'warm-up' exercise, to develop your studies towards the level of full devolved assessment.

(e) Next do the **Trial Run Devolved Assessments**. Although these are not yet fully at the level you can expect when you do a full devolved assessment, they do cover all the performance criteria of the elements indicated.

The AAT have not issued a **Sample Simulation** for Unit 2. Therefore this kit is based on previous simulations under the old syllabus.

Remember this is a **practical** course.

(a) Try to relate the material to your experience in the workplace or any other work experience you may have had.

(b) Try to make as many links as you can to your study of the other units at this level.

UNIT 2 STANDARDS OF COMPETENCE

The structure of the Standards for Unit 2

The Unit commences with a statement of the **knowledge and understanding** which underpin competence in the Unit's elements.

The Unit of Competence is then divided into **elements of competence** describing activities which the individual should be able to perform.

Each element includes:

(a) A set of **performance criteria.** This defines what constitutes competent performance.
(b) A **range statement.** This defines the situations, contexts, methods etc in which competence should be displayed.
(c) **Evidence requirements.** These state that competence must be demonstrated consistently, over an appropriate time scale with evidence of performance being provided from the appropriate sources.
(d) **Sources of evidence.** These are suggestions of ways in which you can find evidence to demonstrate that competence. These fall under the headings: 'observed performance; work produced by the candidate; authenticated testimonies from relevant witnesses; personal account of competence; other sources of evidence.' They are reproduced in full in our Devolved Assessment Kit for Unit 2.

The elements of competence for Unit 2 *Making and Recording Payments* are set out below. Knowledge and understanding required for the unit as a whole are listed first, followed by the performance criteria and range statements for each element. Performance criteria are cross-referenced below to chapters in this Unit 2 *Making and Recording Payments* Interactive Text.

Unit 2: Making and Recording Payments

What is the unit about?

This unit relates to the organisation's expenditure. It includes dealing with documentation from suppliers and ordering and delivery documentation, preparing payments, recording expenditure in the appropriate records, and making payments relating to invoices, wages and salaries, and petty cash.

The first element is concerned with ensuring calculations and records of expenditure are correct and deducting available discounts. It requires the individual to enter documents as primary records and to code and record entries in the appropriate ledgers. The individual is also required to handle both verbal and written communications with suppliers in a polite and effective manner. It should be noted that the individual is not expected to deal with goods supplied under leasing or hire purchase contracts at this level.

The second element relates to preparing authorised payments, relating to creditors, payroll and petty cash. The individual is expected to prepare and analyse payments according to organisational procedures. Any queries on these payments should be referred to the appropriate person.

Maintaining security and confidentiality are key aspects of performance in this element.

The final element relates to the actual making of payments. This involves the individual selecting appropriate payment methods and ensuring that all payments are recorded and entered into the accounting records. This element also requires the individual to take responsibility for ensuring the security of relevant payment methods and to refer queries to the appropriate person.

Knowledge and understanding

The business environment

- Types of business transactions and documents involved (Element 2.1)
- Basic law relating to contract law, Sale of Goods Act and document retention policies (Elements 2.1 and 2.2)
- General principles of VAT (Element 2.1)
- Types of discounts (Element 2.1)
- Automated payments: CHAPS, BACS, direct debits, standing orders (Elements 2.1, 2.2 and 2.3)
- Credit and debit cards (Elements 2.1 and 2.3)
- Different ordering systems: Internet; fax; in writing; telephone (Element 2.1)
- Documentation for payments (Element 2.2)
- Basic law relating to data protection (Element 2.2)
- Legal requirements relating to cheques, including crossing and endorsements (Element 2.3)

Accounting methods

- Double entry bookkeeping (Elements 2.1, 2.2 and 2.3)
- Methods of coding data (Element 2.1)
- Operation of manual and computerised accounting systems (Elements 2.1, 2.2, and 2.3)
- Credit card procedures (Elements 2.1 and 2.3)
- Relationship between accounting system and ledger (Elements 2.1, 2.2 and 2.3)
- Petty cash procedures: imprest and non imprest methods; analysis of items of expenditure including VAT charges (Element 2.2)
- Payroll accounting procedures: accounting for gross pay, statutory and non-statutory deductions and payments to external agencies; security and control; cumulative calculations (Elements 2.2. and 2.3)
- Methods of handling and storing money from a security aspect (Element 2.3)

The organisation

- Relevant understanding of the organisation's accounting systems and administrative systems and procedures (Elements 2.1, 2.2 and 2.3)
- The nature of the organisation's business transactions (Elements 2.1, 2.2 and 2.3)
- Organisational procedures for authorisation and coding of purchase invoices and payments (Element 2.1)
- Organisational procedures for filing source information (Elements 2.1, 2.2 and 2.3)

Unit 2 Standards of Competence

Element 2.1 Process documents relating to goods and services received

Performance criteria		Chapters in the Text
1	Suppliers' invoices and credit notes are checked against delivery notes, ordering documentation and evidence that goods or services have been received	5
2	Totals and balances are correctly calculated and checked on suppliers' invoices	5
3	Available discounts are identified and deducted	5
4	Documents are correctly entered as primary records according to organisational procedures	6
5	Entries are coded and recorded in the appropriate ledger	6, 7
6	Discrepancies are identified and either resolved or referred to the appropriate person if outside own authority	5, 7
7	Communications with suppliers regarding accounts are handled politely and effectively	8
Range statement		
1	Documents: orders; suppliers' invoices; delivery notes; credit notes	5, 6
2	Discounts: trade; settlement	5, 6
3	Primary records: purchase and returns day book	6
4	Ledger: main ledger; subsidiary ledger; integrated ledger	7
5	Discrepancies: incorrect calculations; non-delivery of goods charged; duplicated invoices; incorrect VAT charges; incorrect discounts	5, 8
6	Communications: oral; written	8

Element 2.2 Prepare authorised payments

Performance criteria		Chapters in the Text
1	Payments are correctly calculated from relevant documentation	2, 9
2	Payments are scheduled and authorised by the appropriate person	2, 4, 9
3	Queries are referred to the appropriate person	2
4	Security and confidentiality are maintained according to organisational requirements	2, 9
Range statement		
1	Payments: payroll; creditors; petty cash	2, 4, 9

Unit 2 Standards of Competence

Element 2.3 Make and record payments

Performance criteria	Chapters in the Text
1 The appropriate payment method is used in accordance with organisational procedures	2, 4, 9
2 Payments are made in accordance with organisational processes and timescales	2, 4
3 Payments are entered into accounting records according to organisational procedures	3, 4
4 Queries are referred to the appropriate person	2, 3, 4
5 Security and confidentiality are maintained according to organisational requirements	2
Range statement	
1 Payment methods: cash; cheques; automated payments	2, 4, 9
2 Payment: creditors; wages and salaries; petty cash; cheque requisition form	2, 4, 9
3 Accounting records: cash book	3, 4
4 Queries relating to: unauthorised claims for payment; insufficient supporting evidence; claims exceeding prescribed limit	2, 4

Assessment Strategy

ASSESSMENT STRATEGY

This unit is assessed by **devolved assessment**.

Devolved Assessment

Devolved assessment is a means of collecting evidence of your ability to carry out practical activities and to **operate effectively in the conditions of the workplace** to the standards required. Evidence may be collected at your place of work or at an Approved Assessment Centre by means of simulations of workplace activity, or by a combination of these methods.

If the Approved Assessment Centre is a **workplace** you may be observed carrying out accounting activities as part of your normal work routine. You should collect documentary evidence of the work you have done, or contributed, in an **accounting portfolio**. Evidence collected in a portfolio can be assessed in addition to observed performance or where it is not possible to assess by observation.

Where the Approved Assessment Centre is a **college or training organisation**, devolved assessment will be by means of a combination of the following.

(a) Documentary evidence of activities carried out at the workplace, collected by you in an **accounting portfolio**

(b) Realistic **simulations** of workplace activities; these simulations may take the form of case studies and in-tray exercises and involve the use of primary documents and reference sources

(c) **Projects and assignments** designed to assess the Standards of Competence

If you are unable to provide workplace evidence, you will be able to complete the assessment requirements by the alternative methods listed above.

Possible assessment methods

Where possible, evidence should be collected in the workplace, but this may not be a practical prospect for you. Equally, where workplace evidence can be gathered it may not cover all elements. The AAT regards performance evidence from simulations, case studies, projects and assignments as an acceptable substitute for performance at work, provided that they are based on the Standards and, as far as possible, on workplace practice.

There are a number of methods of assessing accounting competence. The list below is not exhaustive, nor is it prescriptive. Some methods have limited applicability, but others are capable of being expanded to provide challenging tests of competence.

Unit 2 Standards of Competence

Assessment method	Suitable for assessing
Performance of an accounting task either in the workplace or by simulation: eg preparing and processing documents, posting entries, making adjustments, balancing, calculating, analysing information etc by manual or computerised processes	**Basic task competence.** Adding supplementary oral questioning may help to draw out underpinning knowledge and understanding and highlight your ability to deal with contingencies and unexpected occurrences
General case studies. These are broader than simulations. They include more background information about the system and business environment	Ability to **analyse a system** and suggest ways of modifying it. It could take the form of a written report, with or without the addition of oral or written questions
Accounting problems/cases: eg a list of balances that require adjustments and the preparation of final accounts	Understanding of the **general principles of accounting** as applied to a particular case or topic
Preparation of flowcharts/diagrams. To illustrate an actual (or simulated) accounting procedure	**Understanding of the logic** behind a procedure, of controls, and of relationships between departments and procedures. Questions on the flow chart or diagram can provide evidence of underpinning knowledge and understanding
Interpretation of accounting information from an actual or simulated situation. The assessment could include non-financial information and written or oral questioning	**Interpretative competence**
Preparation of written reports on an actual or simulated situation	**Written communication skills**
Analysis of critical incidents, problems encountered, achievements	Your ability to handle **contingencies**
Listing of likely errors eg preparing a list of the main types of errors likely to occur in an actual or simulated procedure	Appreciation of the range of **contingencies** likely to be encountered. Oral or written questioning would be a useful supplement to the list
Outlining the organisation's policies, guidelines and regulations	Performance criteria relating to these aspects of competence. It also provides evidence of competence in **researching information**
Objective tests and short-answer questions	**Specific knowledge**
In-tray exercises	Your **task-management ability** as well as technical competence
Supervisors' reports	**General job competence,** personal effectiveness, reliability, accuracy, and time management. Reports need to be related specifically to the Standards of Competence

Assessment Strategy

Assessment method	Suitable for assessing
Analysis of work logbooks/diaries	**Personal effectiveness,** time management etc. It may usefully be supplemented with oral questioning
Formal written answers to questions	Knowledge and understanding of the **general accounting environment** and its impact on particular units of competence
Oral questioning	**Knowledge and understanding** across the range of competence including organisational procedures, methods of dealing with unusual cases, contingencies and so on. It is often used in conjunction with other methods

Practice devolved assessments

Practice devolved assessment
1 Powell Cars

Performance criteria

The following performance criteria are covered in this Devolved Assessment.

Element 2.2 Prepare authorised payments

1. Payments are correctly calculated from relevant documentation
2. Payments are scheduled and authorised by the appropriate person
3. Queries are referred to the appropriate person
4. Security and confidentiality are maintained according to organisational requirements

Element 2.3 Make and record payments

1. The appropriate payment method is used in accordance with organisational procedures
2. Payments are made in accordance with organisational processes and timescales
3. Payments are entered into accounting records according to organisational procedures
4. Queries are referred to the appropriate person
5. Security and confidentiality are maintained according to organisational requirements

Notes on completing the Assessment

This Assessment is designed to test your ability to prepare petty cash vouchers, record the details in the petty cash book, reconcile to the imprest amount and post the transactions correctly.

You are allowed 3 hours to complete your work

A high level of accuracy is required. Check your work carefully.

Correcting fluid may be used but should be used in moderation. Errors should be crossed out neatly and clearly. You should write in black ink and not in pencil.

A full solution to this Assessment is provided on page 171 of this Kit.

Do not turn to the suggested solution until you have completed all parts of the Assessment.

Practice devolved assessments (data and tasks)

PRACTICE DEVOLVED ASSESSMENT 1: POWELL CARS

Data

Powell Cars is a large car dealership. Approximately 35 people work in the administrative and sales areas and all these people are permitted to use petty cash for sundry expenses. The petty cashier, George Earle, can make payments of up to £100 out of petty cash, which has an imprest amount of £1,000. The petty cashier can authorise expenditure up to £20. Expenditure between £20 and £100 must be authorised by the Office Supervisor, Anne Smeed. Each petty cash form, once completed by the petty cashier, must be signed by the claimant and authorised by the relevant person. Any subsequent changes to the petty cash voucher must be initialled by the person who originally authorised the voucher.

Supporting documentation *should* be provided for all payments from petty cash. In the case of payments involving VAT, a valid VAT invoice must be produced to enable the company to reclaim the tax. Any claim over £20 without supporting documentation must be authorised by the Chief Accountant, Mr A Bowles.

Any member of staff who borrows money from petty cash must return it at the end of the month, before the petty cash book is balanced off or the petty cash is counted. Any payment not appropriate or too large for petty cash may be refused by the petty cashier.

Tasks

Using the documents and information on the following pages, perform the following for the month of April 20X5.

(a) (i) Where appropriate, prepare petty cash vouchers for the receipts and claims made by members of staff with the proper authorisation. Where it would not be appropriate to prepare a petty cash voucher, state what alternative procedures might be followed.

   (ii) Arrange the vouchers in date order and number each one. (The last voucher number in March 20X5 was 1562.) *All* vouchers should be numbered.

(b) Enter the voucher details into the petty cash book.

(c) Reconcile the cash and petty cash vouchers to the imprest amount. Comment on any difference. Balance off the petty cash book at the end of 30 April 20X5.

(d) State the amount necessary to top up the petty cash imprest amount. Prepare a cheque requisition form and a cheque for that amount, with a schedule of notes and coins with which the amount *might* be made up.

(e) Prepare a summary of how the petty cash transactions should be posted, giving code number, name of account and whether the entry is a debit or a credit.

   Note. Any difference in the petty cash reconciliation should be posted to sundry payments.

Documents for use in the solution

The documents for use in the solution come under the following headings.

(a) Blank petty cash vouchers
(b) Cheque requisition form
(c) Blank cheque
(d) Blank petty cash book page

1: Powell Cars

Petty cash vouchers

No _____	No _____
Petty Cash Voucher	**Petty Cash Voucher**
Date _____	Date _____
AMOUNT £ p	AMOUNT £ p
Signature:	Signature:
Authorised by:	Authorised by:

No _____	No _____
Petty Cash Voucher	**Petty Cash Voucher**
Date _____	Date _____
AMOUNT £ p	AMOUNT £ p
Signature:	Signature:
Authorised by:	Authorised by:

No _____	No _____
Petty Cash Voucher	**Petty Cash Voucher**
Date _____	Date _____
AMOUNT £ p	AMOUNT £ p
Signature:	Signature:
Authorised by:	Authorised by:

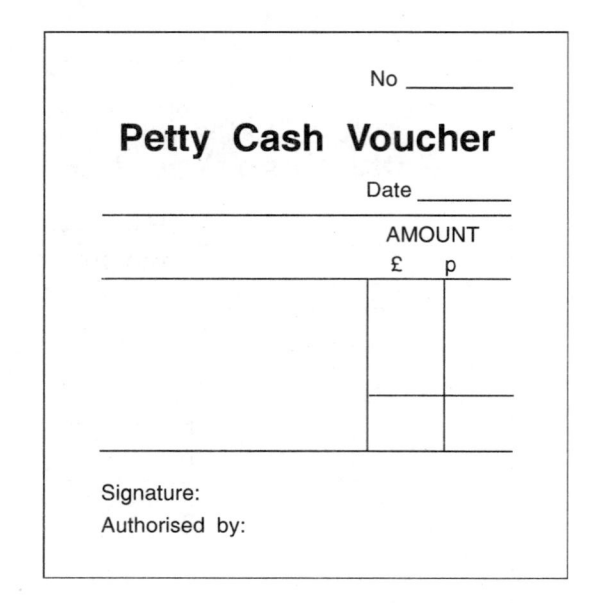

Practice devolved assessments (data and tasks)

Petty Cash Voucher No _____ Date _____ AMOUNT £ p Signature: Authorised by:	**Petty Cash Voucher** No _____ Date _____ AMOUNT £ p Signature: Authorised by:
Petty Cash Voucher No _____ Date _____ AMOUNT £ p Signature: Authorised by:	**Petty Cash Voucher** No _____ Date _____ AMOUNT £ p Signature: Authorised by:
Petty Cash Voucher No _____ Date _____ AMOUNT £ p Signature: Authorised by:	**Petty Cash Voucher** No _____ Date _____ AMOUNT £ p Signature: Authorised by:

1: Powell Cars

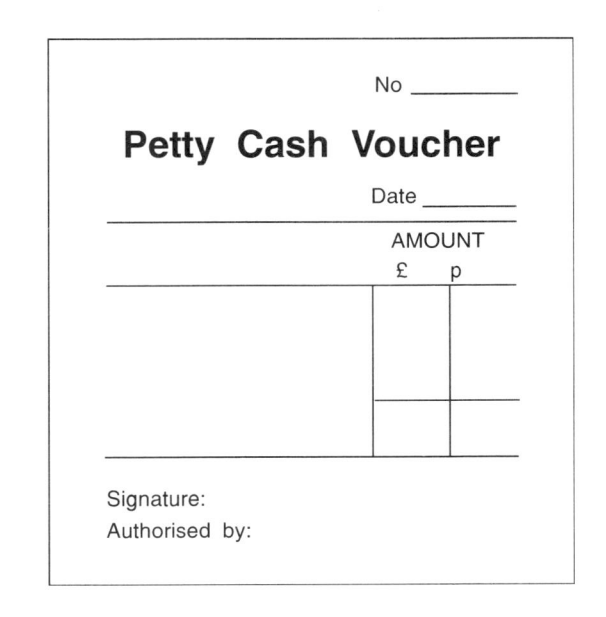

Petty Cash Voucher	Petty Cash Voucher
No _____ Date _____ AMOUNT £ p	No _____ Date _____ AMOUNT £ p
Signature: Authorised by:	Signature: Authorised by:
Petty Cash Voucher	Petty Cash Voucher
No _____ Date _____ AMOUNT £ p	No _____ Date _____ AMOUNT £ p
Signature: Authorised by:	Signature: Authorised by:
Petty Cash Voucher	Petty Cash Voucher
No _____ Date _____ AMOUNT £ p	No _____ Date _____ AMOUNT £ p
Signature: Authorised by:	Signature: Authorised by:

Practice devolved assessments (data and tasks)

Cheque requisition form

```
                                                    247323
            Cheque Requisition

    Date     .................................................
    Payable to .................................................
    Amount   .................................................
    Details  .................................................
             .................................................
             .................................................
    Signed   .................................................
```

Cheque

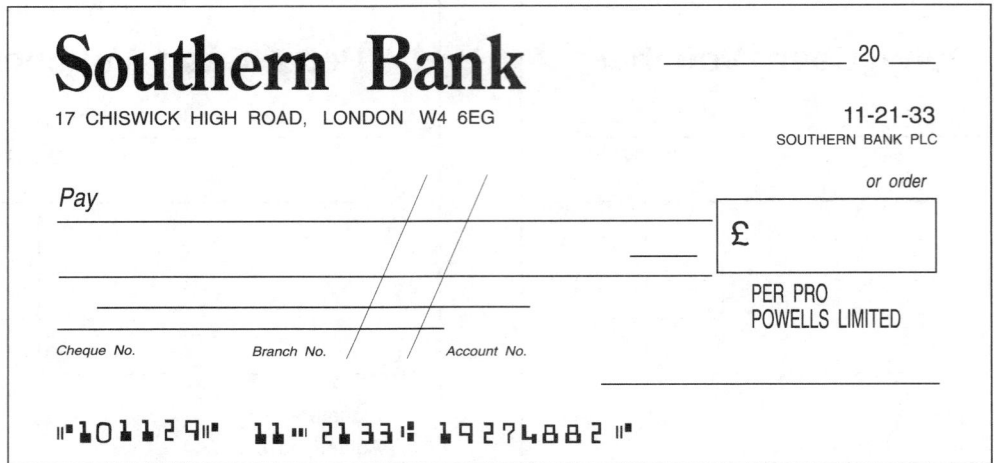

1: Powell Cars

Petty cash book page

PETTY CASH BOOK

Details	Net receipt £	VAT £	Total £	Date	Details	Voucher No	Total £	Analysis of payments					
								Travel £	Postage & stationery £	Staff welfare £	Office supplies £	Sundry £	VAT £

Practice devolved assessments (data and tasks)

Petty cash transactions during April 20X5

The following petty cash details are relevant for April 20X5.

(a) Petty cash claims
(b) Cash count on 30 April 20X5
(c) Ledger account codes

(a) The following have been claimed from petty cash during April.

Petty cash claims

T Goodman: travel to Motor Show 21 April 20X5

	£
Train	68.00
Taxi	24.50
	92.50

C Chappell: travel to Motor Show 21 April 20X5

	£
Train	68.00
Taxi	18.30
	86.30

M Jackson: travel to Motor Show 21 April 20X5

	£
Train	68.00
Taxi	5.00
	73.00

3/4/X5
Office cleaner

Pay £15-00

M Jones.

10/4/X5
Office cleaner

Pay £15-00

P. Clark

17/4/X5
Office cleaner

Pay £15-00

P. Clark

24/4/X5
Office cleaner

Pay £15-00

M Jones.

Buyer's Supermarket

15 04 X5

Coffee x3	4.52
Tea x2	5.25
Sugar x2	2.28
Total	12.05

Mary Smith

Johnson's Hardware

2204X5

Polish	5.25
Dusters	3.42
Window Cleaner	2.50
Rubbish bags	8.95
Vacuum bags	10.50
TOTAL	30.62

P Clark

VAT No 32741562

Bentil's Wine Bar
VAT No 41731629

24 April 20X5

Meal for 2   52.78

C. Chappell
Peter Simpson
(subsistence)

COWCREAM DAIRY   14782

3/4/X5

25 pints milk at 39p   £9-75

P Clark

COWCREAM DAIRY   14811

10/4/X5

25 pints milk at 39p
£9.75

P Clark

Practice devolved assessments (data and tasks)

```
COWCREAM DAIRY
                    14859

              17/4/X5

        25 pints milk
at 39p
              £9-75

            P Clark
```

```
COWCREAM DAIRY
                    14883

              24/4/X5

        20 pints milk
at 39p
              £7-80

            P Clark
```

POST OFFICE	11562347	
8/4/X5		
30 first class stamps	8	10
50 second class stamps	9	50
M. Jones		
	17	60

6 first class stamps taken

6 x 27p = £1.62 paid into petty cash

C. Chappell
6/4/X5

I owe petty cash £10.00

J Smith
15/4/X5

JOHNSON'S HARDWARE

0904X5

LIGHT BULBS
10 X 95P   9.50

TOTAL   9.50

L. Stuart

VAT NO 327 415 62

WRIGHT'S GARAGE

TO: Powell's Limited 30, Rush Green London SW6	INVOICE: 11742 DATE: 3004X5 TAX POINT: 3004X5	
VAT NO 466 211 51		
Repairs Ford Escort Labour 3 hours x £40.50 Parts	121 27	50 32
VAT 17.5% *M Smythe*	148 26	82 04
	174	86

DAWES STATIONERS

INVOICE 3207

DATE: **28 APRIL 20X5**
TAX POINT: **28 APRIL 20X5**

	£
2 x folio cash books @ 28.75	57.50
6 x shorthand notebooks @ £1.25	7.50
2 x box black biros @ £3.60	7.20
1 x hole punch	3.75
	75.95
VAT @ 17.5%	13.29
	89.24

VAT NO 2271 86 38

(b) At the end of 30 April, after all vouchers had been completed and all other necessary procedures followed, the petty cash remaining was counted and the result of the count was as follows.

£20 notes	×	11
£10 notes	×	10
£5 notes	×	12
£1 coins	×	37
50p coins	×	23
20p coins	×	33
10p coins	×	12
5p coins	×	9
2p coins	×	4
1p coins	×	2

(c) The following ledger accounts codes are applicable.

Account	Code
Petty cash	2000
Print, post and stationery	1205
Travel	1315
Staff welfare	1290
Office supplies	1340
Sundry	1395
VAT	7000
Sundry income	3400

Practice devolved assessment 2 Ives

Performance criteria

The following performance criteria are covered in this Devolved Assessment.

Element 2.1 Process documents relating to goods and services received

3 Available discounts are identified and deducted

Element 2.2 Prepare authorised payments

1 Payments are correctly calculated from relevant documentation
2 Payments are scheduled and authorised by the appropriate person
3 Queries are referred to the appropriate person
4 Security and confidentiality are maintained according to organisational requirements

Element 2.3 Make and record payments

1 The appropriate payment method is used in accordance with organisational procedures
2 Payments are made in accordance with organisational processes and timescales
3 Payments are entered into accounting records according to organisational procedures
4 Queries are referred to the appropriate person
5 Security and confidentiality are maintained according to organisational requirements

Notes on completing the Assessment

This Assessment is designed to test your ability to make payments by various means and to record such payments in the ledger.

You are allowed 3 hours to complete your work

A high level of accuracy is required. Check your work carefully.

Correcting fluid may be used but should be used in moderation. Errors should be crossed out neatly and clearly. You should write in black ink, not in pencil.

A full solution to this Assessment is provided on page 179 of this Kit.

Do not turn to the suggested solution until you have completed all parts of the Assessment.

Practice devolved assessment (data and tasks)

PRACTICE DEVOLVED ASSESSMENT 2: IVES

Data

Ives plc is a company which was established nearly a hundred years ago. It manufactures and sells party paper products such as paper napkins, bun cases and other similar products. Paper is bought in bulk, along with dyes and sundry other ingredients. The factory and administrative offices are on the same site on the outskirts of a large Midlands town. Purchases are usually made from about a dozen suppliers, but occasionally purchases have to be made from other sources if the usual suppliers experience shortages. The company runs its own fleet of delivery vans, but urgent deliveries may sometimes be made using an external delivery firm. The company employs five sales representatives who travel the country attempting to sell the company's products to new and existing customers.

The company follows individual policies of paying suppliers, depending on the terms offered by each one. Suppliers' statements are reviewed on a weekly basis and payments are made where required.

Expenses for overheads (gas, electricity, telephones, insurance and so on) are paid by direct debit or standing order where possible.

The following members of staff/management can authorise expenditure according to the table laid out below.

Mr G H Chester	Chairman	Mr R Banner	Purchasing Director
Mr P Hogwood	Managing Director	Mr T Jones	Sales Director
Mrs K Latch	Production Director	Mrs S Smith	Finance Manager
Miss S Chapman	Finance Director	Mr G Taper	Factory Manager

Limit on expenditure	Department/Authority			
	Purchasing	*Production*	*Sales*	*Finance*
No limit	Chairman and Managing Director	Chairman and Managing Director	Chairman and Managing Director	Chairman and Managing Director
£25,000	Purchasing Director and Finance Director	Production Director and Finance Director	Sales Director and Finance Director	Finance Director and Finance Director
£15,000	Purchasing Director	Production Director	Sales Director	Finance Director
£500	Factory Manager	Factory Manager	Finance Manager	Finance Manager

Cheques can only be prepared from *authorised* supporting documentation. Cheques are signed by the Finance Director (if under £25,000) or by the Finance Director and Managing Director (if over £25,000).

Tasks

Using the documents and information on the following pages, complete the tasks outlined below for 29 May 20X5.

(a) (i) Examine the suppliers' statements shown and determine the amounts to be paid to each, according to the forms shown. Obtain any necessary authorisation. Prepare a payments schedule.

(ii) Prepare remittance advices for each of the payments determined in (a) (i).

Note. You should set off any credit notes against the most recent preceding invoices for the purposes of calculating the discount, unless stated otherwise.

(b) (i) Examine the expenses claim forms submitted by the sales representatives, and obtain any further information and any authorisation required. State what supporting documentation would be required with the expenses claim forms.

(ii) Prepare cheque requisition forms for each of the expense claims.

(c) State who should give authorisation and check details on the invoices received for sundry purchases, overheads and expenses. Prepare remittance advices for each payment.

(d) Prepare cheques for all the payments noted in (a), (b) and (c). Cross all the cheques to suppliers 'Not negotiable'.

(e) (i) Prepare a new standing order mandate for the company's insurance payments.

(ii) State the differences between making payments by standing order and by direct debit.

(f) Fill in the request form for a banker's draft to pay for the Chairman's new company car.

(g) The salesman, D Hill, is found to have been defrauding the company by claiming twice as much petrol as he has actually purchased (using false receipts). You are instructed to stop the cheque paid to him for his expenses as he has now been dismissed. Show how you would carry out this instruction (showing any letters etc written).

(h) Write up the payments side of the cash book for 29 May 20X5, to reflect the transactions shown above and the bank statements dated 3 June 20X5. (*Note.* Think carefully about how you should use the analysis columns.)

Note: VAT should be rounded up or down to the nearest penny.

Documents for use in the solution

The documents you will need to prepare a solution are given on the following pages and consist of:

(a) remittance advices
(b) cheque requisition forms
(c) cheques
(d) a standing order mandate form
(e) a cash book page
(f) a banker's draft request form

Practice devolved assessment (data and tasks)

Remittance advices

14723				
REMITTANCE ADVICE TO:		IVES PLC Works Lane Walsall 01922 42731		
Account Ref	Date		Page	
DATE	DETAILS	INVOICES	CREDIT NOTES	PAYMENT AMOUNT

14724				
REMITTANCE ADVICE TO:		IVES PLC Works Lane Walsall 01922 42731		
Account Ref	Date		Page	
DATE	DETAILS	INVOICES	CREDIT NOTES	PAYMENT AMOUNT

14725

REMITTANCE ADVICE

TO:

IVES PLC
Works Lane
Walsall
01922 42731

Account Ref		Date		Page	

DATE	DETAILS	INVOICES	CREDIT NOTES	PAYMENT AMOUNT

14726

REMITTANCE ADVICE

TO:

IVES PLC
Works Lane
Walsall
01922 42731

Account Ref		Date		Page	

DATE	DETAILS	INVOICES	CREDIT NOTES	PAYMENT AMOUNT

14727

REMITTANCE ADVICE

TO:

IVES PLC
Works Lane
Walsall
01922 42731

| Account Ref | | Date | | Page | |

DATE	DETAILS	INVOICES	CREDIT NOTES	PAYMENT AMOUNT

14728

REMITTANCE ADVICE

TO:

IVES PLC
Works Lane
Walsall
01922 42731

| Account Ref | | Date | | Page | |

DATE	DETAILS	INVOICES	CREDIT NOTES	PAYMENT AMOUNT

14729					
REMITTANCE ADVICE			IVES PLC		
TO:			Works Lane		
			Walsall		
			01922 42731		

Account Ref [ ]   Date [ ]   Page [ ]

DATE	DETAILS	INVOICES	CREDIT NOTES	PAYMENT AMOUNT

14730					
REMITTANCE ADVICE			IVES PLC		
TO:			Works Lane		
			Walsall		
			01922 42731		

Account Ref [ ]   Date [ ]   Page [ ]

DATE	DETAILS	INVOICES	CREDIT NOTES	PAYMENT AMOUNT

14731

REMITTANCE ADVICE

TO:

IVES PLC
Works Lane
Walsall
01922 42731

| Account Ref | | Date | | Page | |

DATE	DETAILS	INVOICES	CREDIT NOTES	PAYMENT AMOUNT

14732

REMITTANCE ADVICE

TO:

IVES PLC
Works Lane
Walsall
01922 42731

| Account Ref | | Date | | Page | |

DATE	DETAILS	INVOICES	CREDIT NOTES	PAYMENT AMOUNT

14733

REMITTANCE ADVICE

TO:

IVES PLC
Works Lane
Walsall
01922 42731

Account Ref		Date		Page	

DATE	DETAILS	INVOICES	CREDIT NOTES	PAYMENT AMOUNT

14734

REMITTANCE ADVICE

TO:

IVES PLC
Works Lane
Walsall
01922 42731

Account Ref		Date		Page	

DATE	DETAILS	INVOICES	CREDIT NOTES	PAYMENT AMOUNT

14735

REMITTANCE ADVICE

TO:

IVES PLC
Works Lane
Walsall
01922 42731

| Account Ref | | Date | | Page | |

DATE	DETAILS	INVOICES	CREDIT NOTES	PAYMENT AMOUNT

14736

REMITTANCE ADVICE

TO:

IVES PLC
Works Lane
Walsall
01922 42731

| Account Ref | | Date | | Page | |

DATE	DETAILS	INVOICES	CREDIT NOTES	PAYMENT AMOUNT

14737				
REMITTANCE ADVICE TO:		IVES PLC Works Lane Walsall 01922 42731		
Account Ref		Date	Page	
DATE	DETAILS	INVOICES	CREDIT NOTES	PAYMENT AMOUNT

Cheque requisition forms

Cheque Requisition — 247320

Date ....
Payable to ....
Amount ....
Details ....
....
....
Signed ....

Cheque Requisition — 247321

Date ....
Payable to ....
Amount ....
Details ....
....
....
Signed ....

Practice devolved assessment (data and tasks)

Cheque Requisition 247322

Date ....
Payable to ....
Amount ....
Details ....
....
....
Signed ....

Cheque Requisition 247323

Date ....
Payable to ....
Amount ....
Details ....
....
....
Signed ....

Cheque Requisition 247324

Date ....
Payable to ....
Amount ....
Details ....
....
....
Signed ....

Cheques

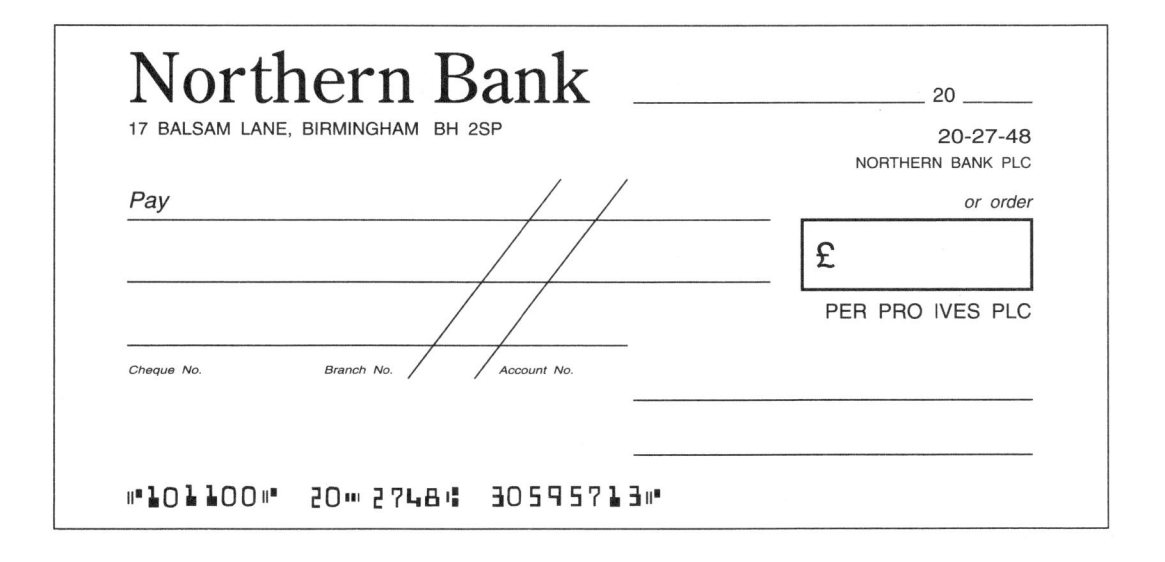

Northern Bank
17 BALSAM LANE, BIRMINGHAM BH 2SP

_____ 20 _____

20-27-48
NORTHERN BANK PLC

Pay _____ or order

£ [   ]

PER PRO IVES PLC

Cheque No.   Branch No.   Account No.

⑈101100⑈ 20⑈2748⑉ 30595713⑈

Northern Bank
17 BALSAM LANE, BIRMINGHAM BH 2SP

_____ 20 _____

20-27-48
NORTHERN BANK PLC

Pay _____ or order

£ [   ]

PER PRO IVES PLC

Cheque No.   Branch No.   Account No.

⑈101101⑈ 20⑈2748⑉ 30595713⑈

Northern Bank
17 BALSAM LANE, BIRMINGHAM BH 2SP

_____ 20 _____

20-27-48
NORTHERN BANK PLC

Pay _____ or order

£ [   ]

PER PRO IVES PLC

Cheque No.   Branch No.   Account No.

⑈101102⑈ 20⑈2748⑉ 30595713⑈

Practice devolved assessment (data and tasks)

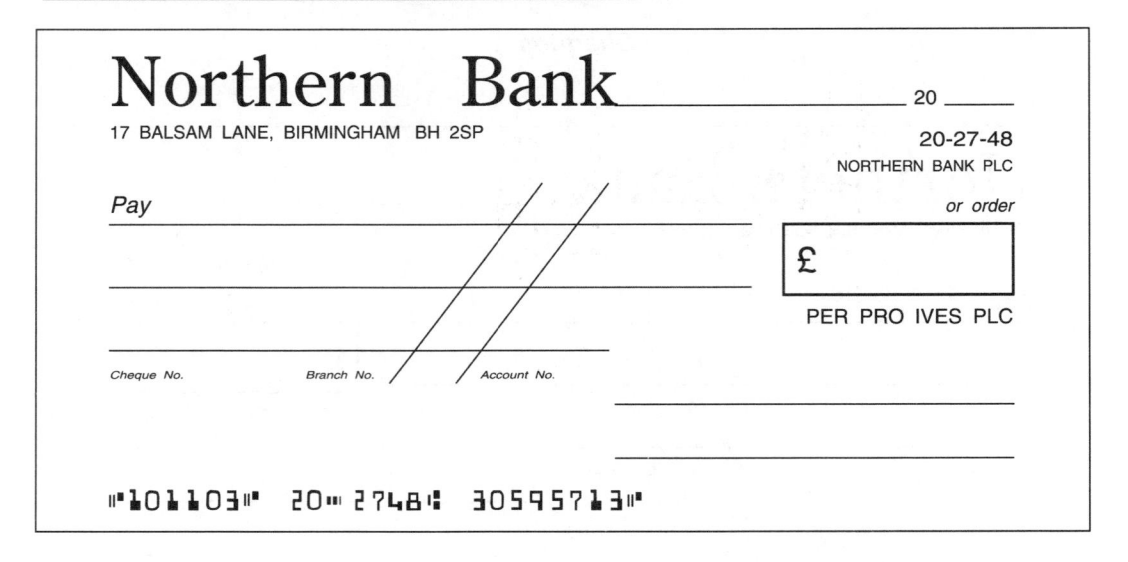

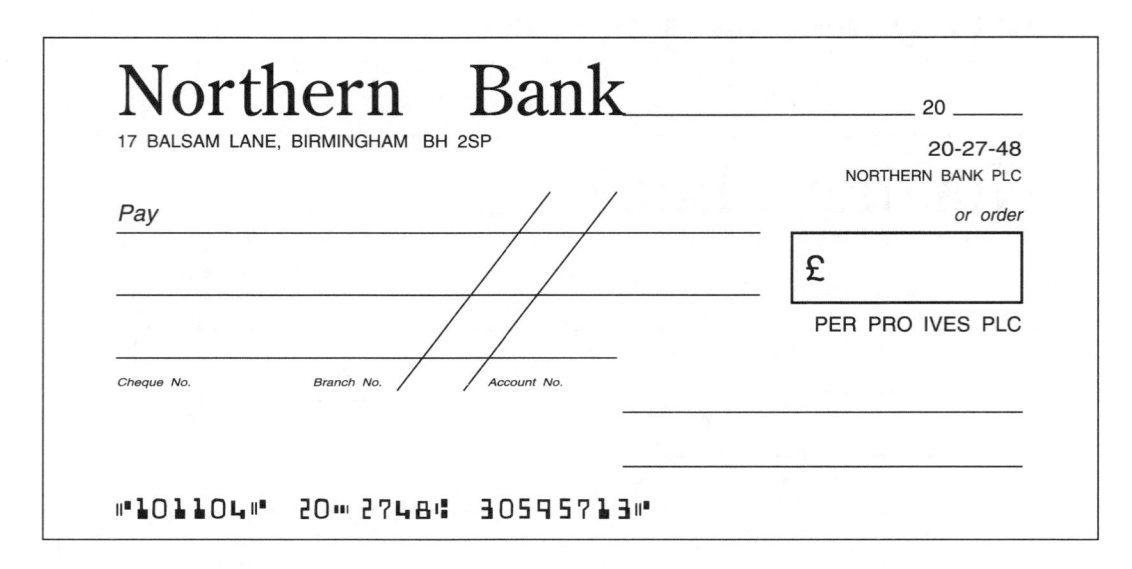

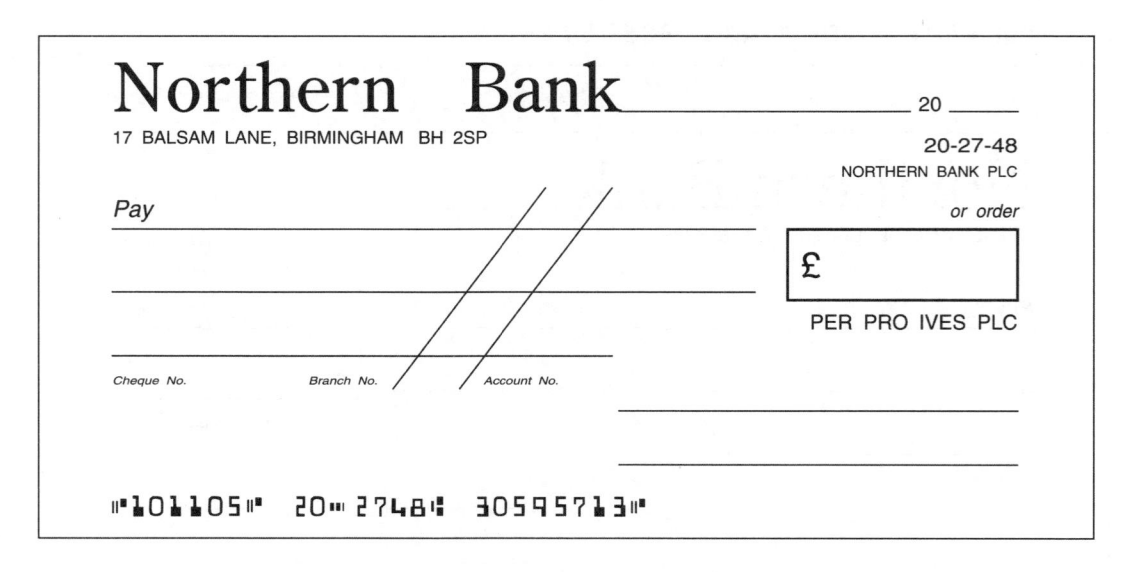

Northern Bank
17 BALSAM LANE, BIRMINGHAM BH 2SP

20 _____

20-27-48
NORTHERN BANK PLC

Pay _____ or order

£ _____

PER PRO IVES PLC

Cheque No.   Branch No.   Account No.

⑈101103⑈ 20⑆2748⑉ 30595713⑈

Northern Bank
17 BALSAM LANE, BIRMINGHAM BH 2SP

20 _____

20-27-48
NORTHERN BANK PLC

Pay _____ or order

£ _____

PER PRO IVES PLC

Cheque No.   Branch No.   Account No.

⑈101104⑈ 20⑆2748⑉ 30595713⑈

Northern Bank
17 BALSAM LANE, BIRMINGHAM BH 2SP

20 _____

20-27-48
NORTHERN BANK PLC

Pay _____ or order

£ _____

PER PRO IVES PLC

Cheque No.   Branch No.   Account No.

⑈101105⑈ 20⑆2748⑉ 30595713⑈

Northern Bank

17 BALSAM LANE, BIRMINGHAM BH 2SP

20 _____

20-27-48
NORTHERN BANK PLC

Pay _____ or order

£

PER PRO IVES PLC

Cheque No.   Branch No.   Account No.

⑊101106⑊ 20⑊2748⑊ 30595713⑊

Northern Bank

17 BALSAM LANE, BIRMINGHAM BH 2SP

20 _____

20-27-48
NORTHERN BANK PLC

Pay _____ or order

£

PER PRO IVES PLC

Cheque No.   Branch No.   Account No.

⑊101107⑊ 20⑊2748⑊ 30595713⑊

Northern Bank

17 BALSAM LANE, BIRMINGHAM BH 2SP

20 _____

20-27-48
NORTHERN BANK PLC

Pay _____ or order

£

PER PRO IVES PLC

Cheque No.   Branch No.   Account No.

⑊101108⑊ 20⑊2748⑊ 30595713⑊

Practice devolved assessment (data and tasks)

Northern Bank
17 BALSAM LANE, BIRMINGHAM BH 2SP

20 _____

20-27-48
NORTHERN BANK PLC

Pay

or order

£

PER PRO IVES PLC

Cheque No.   Branch No.   Account No.

⑈101109⑈ 20⬝2748⑆ 30595713⑈

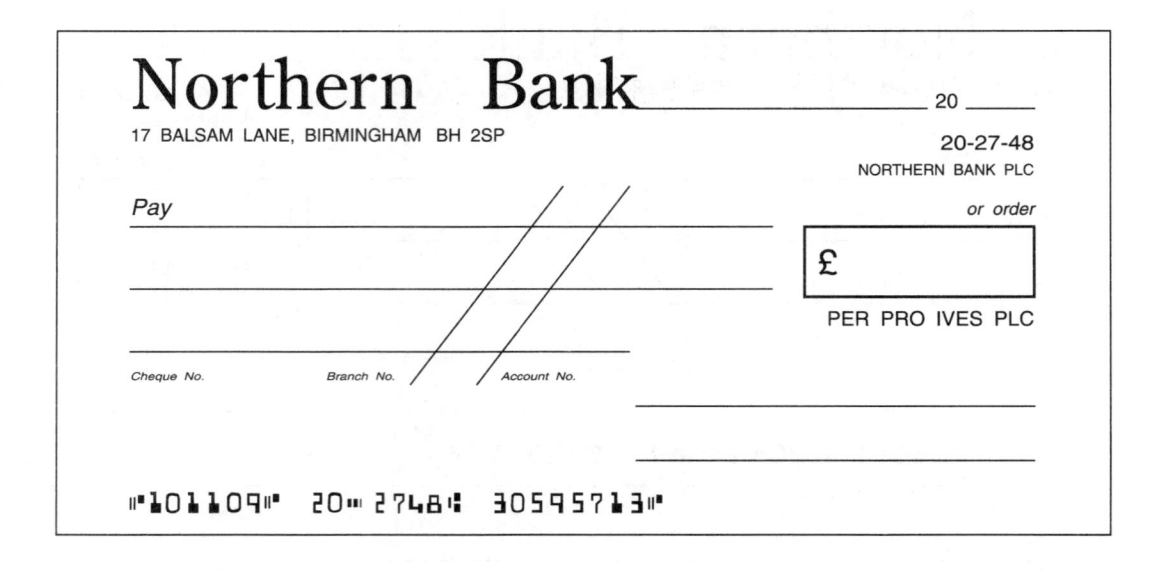

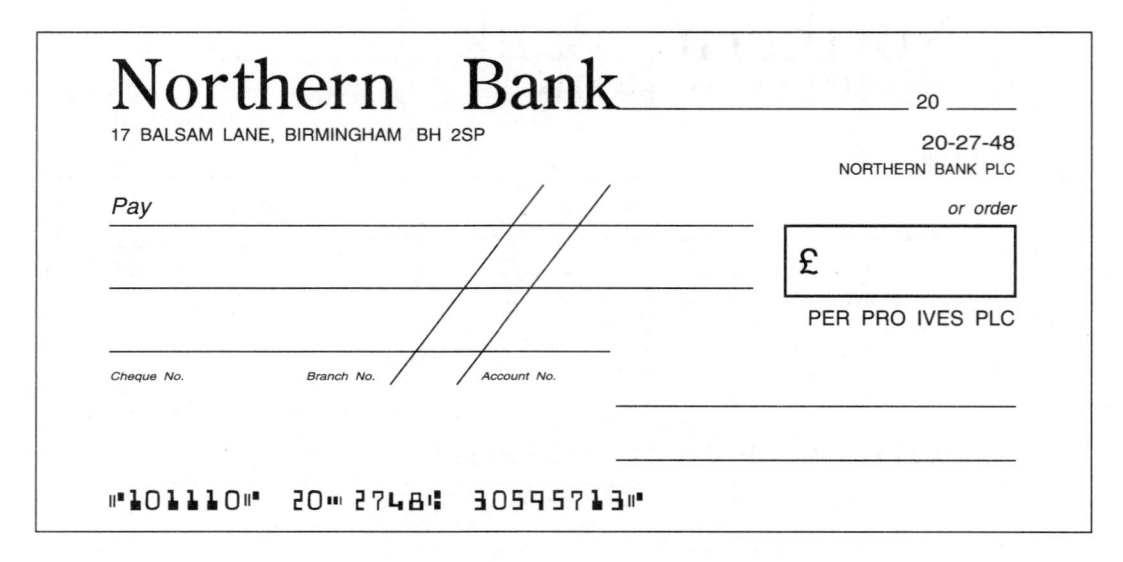

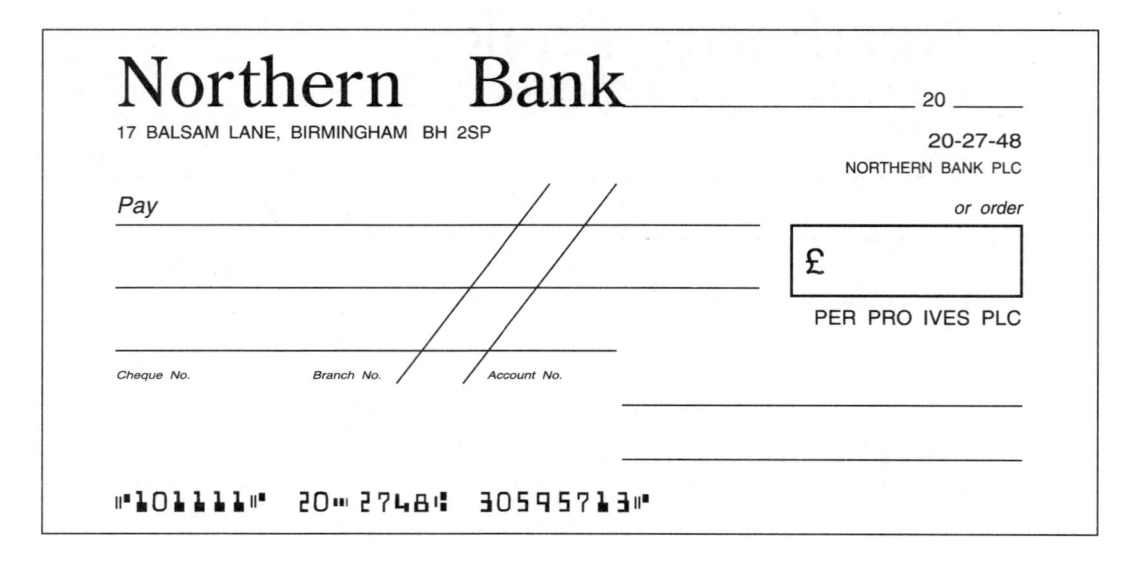

Northern Bank
17 BALSAM LANE, BIRMINGHAM BH 2SP

20 _____

20-27-48
NORTHERN BANK PLC

Pay

or order

£

PER PRO IVES PLC

Cheque No.   Branch No.   Account No.

⑈101110⑈ 20⬝2748⑆ 30595713⑈

Northern Bank
17 BALSAM LANE, BIRMINGHAM BH 2SP

20 _____

20-27-48
NORTHERN BANK PLC

Pay

or order

£

PER PRO IVES PLC

Cheque No.   Branch No.   Account No.

⑈101111⑈ 20⬝2748⑆ 30595713⑈

Northern Bank

17 BALSAM LANE, BIRMINGHAM BH 2SP   20 _____

                                                                 20-27-48
                                                                 NORTHERN BANK PLC

Pay _____   or order

    _____   [£   ]

    _____   PER PRO IVES PLC

Cheque No.   Branch No.   Account No.

⑈101112⑈ 20⋯2748⑆ 30595713⑈

Northern Bank

17 BALSAM LANE, BIRMINGHAM BH 2SP   20 _____

                                                                 20-27-48
                                                                 NORTHERN BANK PLC

Pay _____   or order

    _____   [£   ]

    _____   PER PRO IVES PLC

Cheque No.   Branch No.   Account No.

⑈101113⑈ 20⋯2748⑆ 30595713⑈

Northern Bank

17 BALSAM LANE, BIRMINGHAM BH 2SP   20 _____

                                                                 20-27-48
                                                                 NORTHERN BANK PLC

Pay _____   or order

    _____   [£   ]

    _____   PER PRO IVES PLC

Cheque No.   Branch No.   Account No.

⑈101114⑈ 20⋯2748⑆ 30595713⑈

Practice devolved assessment (data and tasks)

Northern Bank

17 BALSAM LANE, BIRMINGHAM BH 2SP

_____ 20 _____

20-27-48
NORTHERN BANK PLC

Pay _____ or order

£ [   ]

PER PRO IVES PLC

Cheque No.   Branch No.   Account No.

⑈101115⑈ 20⑆2748⑊ 30595713⑈

Northern Bank

17 BALSAM LANE, BIRMINGHAM BH 2SP

_____ 20 _____

20-27-48
NORTHERN BANK PLC

Pay _____ or order

£ [   ]

PER PRO IVES PLC

Cheque No.   Branch No.   Account No.

⑈101116⑈ 20⑆2748⑊ 30595713⑈

Standing order mandate form

Standing Order Mandate

TO _____ BANK

Address _____

Please pay

Bank	Branch Title (not address)	Sorting Code Number

for the credit of

Beneficiary's Name	Account Number

the sum of

Regular amount in figures	Regular amount in words
£	

commencing

Date and Amount of First Payment	and thereafter every	Due Date and Frequency
£		

*until

Date and Amount of Last Payment
£

*until you receive further notice from me/us in writing and debit my/our account accordingly.

quoting the reference _____

This instruction cancels any previous order in favour of the beneficiary named above, under this reference.

Special instructions:

Account to be debited	Account Number

Signature(s) _____   Date _____

*Delete if not applicable

Cash book page

MAY - PAYMENTS

Date	Details	Cheque number	Discounts received	Total	VAT	Creditors

Purchases	Carriage	Bank charges interest	Telephone	Insurance	Motor expenses	Print, post & stationery	Wages and salaries	Fixed assets	Subsistence & sundry

Practice devolved assessment (data and tasks)

Banker's draft request form

Application for Inland Draft
To Northern Bank Plc

_____ Date _____

Kindly supply a crossed Draft.   *Marked ~~'account payee'~~

Payable to _____

£ _____ amount in words   _____

_____

*Please debit my/our account no   ☐☐☐☐☐☐☐

*~~Herewith cash to cover~~

*~~Herewith cheque to cover~~

Charges (if any) to be   ~~*deducted~~   *Delete as necessary
charged to me/us

Signature(s) _____

Name(s) _____

Address _____
(if not a
customer) _____

I/We acknowledge receipt of the above mentioned Draft numbered _____

_____ Signature

(To be signed by an authorised person in the company and returned to the bank)

Payments transactions for 29 May 20X5

The payments transactions which took place on 29 May 20X5 are listed under the following headings.

(a) Suppliers' statements received, terms taken and supplier account codes
(b) Expenses claim forms
(c) Sundry invoices received
(d) Mr Chester's new company car
(e) Insurance charges for the next year
(f) Bank statement dated 3 June 20X5

Suppliers' statements, terms taken, and account codes for Ives plc's records

Barton Bulk Paper: take 3% discount for payment within 7 days. Account code B001.

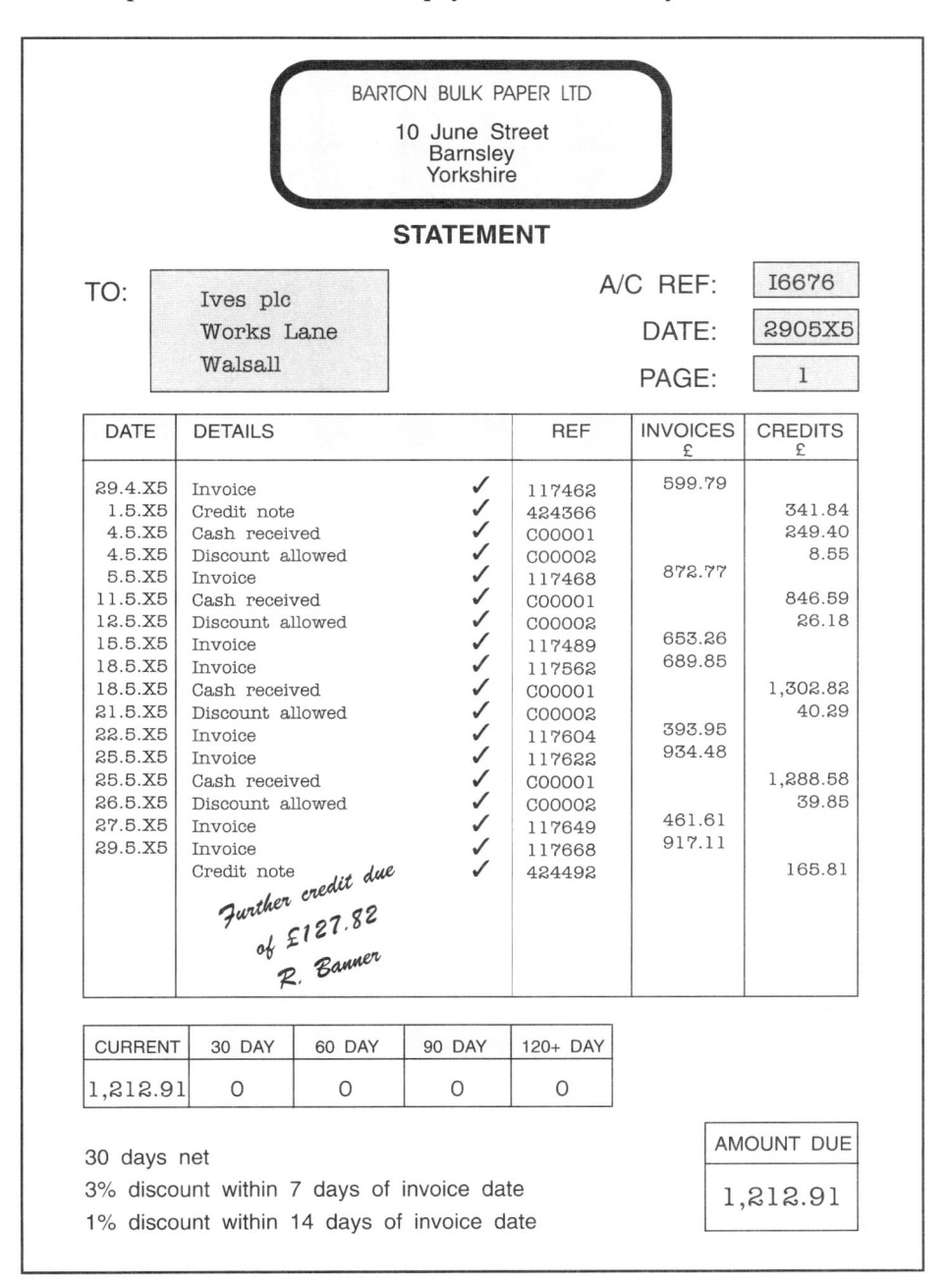

BARTON BULK PAPER LTD
10 June Street
Barnsley
Yorkshire

STATEMENT

TO: Ives plc, Works Lane, Walsall

A/C REF: I6676
DATE: 2905X5
PAGE: 1

DATE	DETAILS		REF	INVOICES £	CREDITS £
29.4.X5	Invoice	✓	117462	599.79	
1.5.X5	Credit note	✓	424366		341.84
4.5.X5	Cash received	✓	C00001		249.40
4.5.X5	Discount allowed	✓	C00002		8.55
5.5.X5	Invoice	✓	117468	872.77	
11.5.X5	Cash received	✓	C00001		846.59
12.5.X5	Discount allowed	✓	C00002		26.18
15.5.X5	Invoice	✓	117489	653.26	
18.5.X5	Invoice	✓	117562	689.85	
18.5.X5	Cash received	✓	C00001		1,302.82
21.5.X5	Discount allowed	✓	C00002		40.29
22.5.X5	Invoice	✓	117604	393.95	
25.5.X5	Invoice	✓	117622	934.48	
25.5.X5	Cash received	✓	C00001		1,288.58
26.5.X5	Discount allowed	✓	C00002		39.85
27.5.X5	Invoice	✓	117649	461.61	
29.5.X5	Invoice	✓	117668	917.11	
	Credit note	✓	424492		165.81

Further credit due of £127.82
R. Banner

CURRENT	30 DAY	60 DAY	90 DAY	120+ DAY
1,212.91	0	0	0	0

30 days net
3% discount within 7 days of invoice date
1% discount within 14 days of invoice date

AMOUNT DUE: 1,212.91

Practice devolved assessment (data and tasks)

Drips Industrial Dyes: pay within terms, no discount. Account code: D001.

Drips Industrial Dyes
44 Wain Estate
Walsall

STATEMENT

DATE: 2905X5

TO: Ives plc
Works Lane
Walsall

A/C REF: 117428

PAGE: 1

DATE	DETAILS		INVOICES	CREDITS
1.5.X5	Invoice S42738	✓	53 50	
2.5.X5	Invoice S42742	✓	30 90	
6.5.X5	Invoice S42783	✓	30 90	
8.5.X5	C/Note C42801	✓		22 60
10.5.X5	Invoice S42829	✓	92 70	
14.5.X5	Invoice S42856	✓	56 60	
21.5.X5	Invoice S42911	✓	30 90	
23.5.X5	Invoice S42934	✓	56 60	
24.5.X5	Invoice S42940	✓	113 20	
29.5.X5	Invoice S42971	✓	87 50	
	R Banner			
			552 80	22 60

Terms: 30 days net

CURRENT	30 DAY	60 DAY	90 DAY	120+ DAY
£530.20	0	0	0	0

AMOUNT DUE

£530.20

Mache Paper plc: take 2½% discount for payment within 14 days. Account code M001.

Mache Paper plc
Black Country Trading Estate
Birmingham
0121 546 2713

STATEMENT

DATE: 2805X5
A/C REF: 173271
PAGE: 1

TO: Ives plc
Works Lane
Walsall

DATE	DETAILS	AMOUNT	BALANCE
14.2.X5	Invoice 4270937	1,774.81	1,774.81
17.2.X5	Invoice 4271089	2,079.23	3,854.04
28.2.X5	Unallocated cash	-3,408.41	445.63
26.3.X5	Invoice 4272150	2,957.92	3,403.55
27.3.X5	Invoice 4272168	1,619.25	5,022.80
31.3.X5	Unallocated cash	-4,244.62	778.18
15.5.X5	Invoice 4274842 ✓	3,091.12	3,869.30
20.5.X5	Invoice 4275204 ✓	1,584.47	5,453.77
27.5.X5	Invoice 4275432 ✓	4,217.14	9,670.91
28.5.X5	Credit note 5881729 ✓	-327.88	9,343.03

February and March invoices still in dispute

R. Banner

Terms
30 days net   2.5% discount if paid within 14 days of invoice date

CURRENT	30 DAY	60 DAY	90 DAY	120+ DAY
8,564.85	0	332.55	445.63	0

AMOUNT DUE
£9,343.03

Practice devolved assessment (data and tasks)

Rainbow Dyes Ltd: pay within terms, no discount. Account code R001.

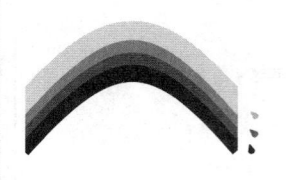

Rainbow Dyes Ltd
14, Rothside Road
Birmingham

STATEMENT

TO: Ives plc
Works Lane
Walsall   l4217

DATE: 2805X5
PAGE: 1

Date	Details		Invoices	Credits	Balance
0105X5	Invoice 401136	✓	137.00		137.00
0505X5	Invoice 401192	✓	171.25		308.25
0705X5	Invoice 401235	✓	102.75		411.00
1405X5	Credit note C6374	✓		68.50	342.50
1505X5	Invoice 401317	✓	274.00		616.50
1905X5	Invoice 401389	✓	102.75		719.25
2205X5	Invoice 401442	✓	137.00		856.25
2605X5	Invoice 401470	✓	239.75		1,096.00
2805X5	Credit note C6428	✓		102.75	993.25
2805X5	Invoice 401522	✓	171.25		1,164.50

R. Banner

CURRENT	30 DAY	60 DAY	90+ DAY
1,164.50	0	0	0

AMOUNT DUE
1,164.50

TERMS: 30 days net

Wright Wrappings: pay within terms, no discount. Account code W001.

```
Wright Wrappings                                    STATEMENT

34 George's Yard, Manchester

TO:    Ives plc        A/C REF:  1042       DATE:   25/5/X5
       Works Lane
       Walsall                               PAGE:   1
```

DATE	DETAILS		
1/5/X5	Invoice 12423 ✓		127.52
13/5/X5	Invoice 12451 ✓		141.80
20/5/X5	Invoice 12493 ✓		92.63
25/5/X5	Invoice 12520 ✓		58.22
			420.17

G Taper

AMOUNT DUE
420.17

TERMS: 30 days net

Practice devolved assessment (data and tasks)

Linton Paper Co: 1½% discount for payment within 14 days. Account code L001.

Linton Paper Co
Kemp Trading Estate
Birmingham

STATEMENT

DATE: 2805X5

A/C REF: I1234

TO: Ives plc
Works Lane
Walsall

PAGE: 1

DATE	DETAILS	REF	£
1304X5	Invoice	10732492	1,792.18
1504X5	Invoice	10733218	2,957.91
1604X5	Invoice	10733970	2,036.73
2204X5	Invoice	10734869	4,892.65
2404X5	Cash received	R0740162	(6,685.02)
2804X5	Invoice	10735244	1,893.55
0105X5	Cash received	R0751426	(4,819.26)
0505X5	Invoice	10735976	5,465.66
0805X5	Cash received	R0752117	(1,865.15)
1105X5	Invoice	10736114	1,040.25
1405X5	Invoice	10736387	2,793.25
1505X5	Cash received	R0752841	(5,383.68)
1805X5	Invoice	10736509 ✓	3,721.59
2005X5	Invoice	10736615 ✓	2,632.56
2105X5	Invoice	10736692 ✓	7,789.17
2205X5	Cash received *G H Chester*	R0752996	(3,776.00)
2505X5	Invoice	10737047 ✓	4,824.96
2705X5	Invoice *P Hogwood*	10737222 ✓	2,167.85
2805X5	Invoice	10737514 ✓	7,778.85
	Discounts taken		
2404X5	1.5% x 6,786.82		(101.80)
0105X5	1.5% x 4,892.65		(73.39)
0805X5	1.5% x 1,893.55		(28.40)
1505X5	1.5% x 5,465.66		(81.98)
2205X5	1.5% x 3,833.50		(57.50)

CURRENT	30 DAY	60 DAY
28,914.98	0	0

Amount Due

£28,914.98

TERMS
30 days net
1.5% discount within 14 days of invoice

Bright Dyes Ltd: take 2% discount for payment within 14 days. Account code B002.

	STATEMENT	28 May 20X5		**Bright Dyes Ltd** 437 Tilley Hill Newcastle-upon-Tyne
TO:	Ives plc Works Lane Walsall		A/C REF: 432117 PAGE: 1	

DATE	DETAILS			INVOICES	CREDITS	BALANCE
6 May X5	Invoice	TN143284	✓	411.60		411.60
8 May X5	Credit note	CN143301	✓		411.60	0
17 May X5	Invoice	TN143517	✓	740.88		740.88
18 May X5	Invoice	TN143642	✓	246.96		987.84
21 May X5	Invoice	TN143739	✓	329.28		1,317.12
25 May X5	Invoice	TN143890	✓	164.64		1,481.76
26 May X5	Invoice	TN143944	✓	82.32		1,564.08
28 May X5	Invoice	TN144086	✓	493.92		2,058.00

R. Banner

TERMS
30 days net
2% discount within 14 days of invoice

AMOUNT DUE

2,058.00

Practice devolved assessment (data and tasks)

Prior Paper Products Ltd: pay within terms, no discount. Account code P001.

Prior Papers Products Ltd
4 Berry Street
Liverpool

STATEMENT

TO: Ives plc
Works Lane
Walsall

DATE: 2805X5

A/C REF: O1171 PAGE: 1

DATE	DETAILS		INVOICES £	CREDITS £
02.04.X5	Invoice I1724057	✓	393.95	
06.04.X5	Invoice I1724322	✓	482.96	
08.04.X5	Invoice I1724509	✓	120.78	
15.04.X5	Credit note (Invoice I1723112)	✓		28.70
17.04.X5	Invoice I1724814	✓	261.61	
22.04.X5	Invoice I1725072	✓	167.04	
24.04.X5	Invoice I1725159	✓	209.81	
28.04.X5	Credit note (Invoice I1724322)	✓		68.57
01.05.X5	Invoice I1725380	✓	380.65	
06.05.X5	Invoice I1725442	✓	377.67	
08.05.X5	Invoice I1725589	✓	631.52	
12.05.X5	Invoice I1725710	✓	70.15	
15.05.X5	Invoice I1725846	✓	194.77	
19.05.X5	Invoice I1725994	✓	108.49	
25.05.X5	Credit note (Invoice I1724322)	✓		49.84
26.05.X5	Credit note (Invoice I1725589)	✓		57.51
	R Banner		3,399.40	204.62

CURRENT	30 DAY	60 DAY	AMOUNT DUE
1,655.90	1,538.88		£3,194.78

TERMS: 30 days net

Expenses claim forms

Note. All claims for meals were subsistence expenses, not entertaining.

Expenses claim form

Name: D. Hill   Month: May
Department: Sales

	Nominal ledger code	NET £	VAT £	TOTAL £
MOTOR CAR EXPENSES				
Petrol		122.45	21.43	143.88
Repairs and service		104.82	18.34	123.16
Parking		6.20		6.20
Car tax				
		233.47	39.77	273.24
OTHER TRAVEL COSTS				
(Specify) Taxi		8.50		8.50
TELEPHONE EXPENSES				
(Attach telephone bill)		43.20	7.56	50.76
OTHER				
(Entertaining, subsistence etc)		52.30	9.15	61.45
TOTAL CLAIMED Dinner (3 nights)		337.47	56.48	393.95

Signature of claimant: D. Hill   Date: 29 May 20X5
Authorised by: ....   Date: ....

Expenses claim form

Name: R Chalmers   Month: May
Department: Sales

	Nominal ledger code	NET £	VAT £	TOTAL £
MOTOR CAR EXPENSES				
Petrol		207.95	36.39	244.34
Repairs and service				
Parking		21.70		21.70
Car tax				
		229.65	36.39	266.04
OTHER TRAVEL COSTS				
(Specify) Taxi		10.00		10.00
TELEPHONE EXPENSES				
(Attach telephone bill)		22.57	3.95	26.52
OTHER				
(Entertaining, subsistence etc)		78.92	13.81	92.73
TOTAL CLAIMED Dinner (5 nights)		341.14	54.15	395.29

Signature of claimant: R Chalmers   Date: 28 May 20X5
Authorised by: T Jones   Date: 29 May 20X5

Practice devolved assessment (data and tasks)

Expenses claim form

Name: *Linda Graves* Month: *May*

Department: *Sales*

	Nominal ledger code	NET £	VAT £	TOTAL £
MOTOR CAR EXPENSES				
Petrol		106.96	18.72	125.68
Repairs and service		43.19	7.56	50.75
Parking		55.00	-	55.00
Car tax				
		205.15	26.28	231.43
OTHER TRAVEL COSTS				
(Specify) *Train (Leeds)*		21.61		21.61
TELEPHONE EXPENSES				
(Attach telephone bill)				
OTHER				
(Entertaining, subsistence etc)		91.56	16.02	107.58
Dinner (6 nights)				
TOTAL CLAIMED		318.32	42.30	360.62

Signature of claimant: *L. Graves*   Date: *28/5/X5*

Authorised by: *T Jones*   Date: *29 May 20X5*

Expenses claim form

Name: *C Prior*   Month: *May*

Department: *Sales*

	Nominal ledger code	NET £	VAT £	TOTAL £
MOTOR CAR EXPENSES				
Petrol		87.40	15.30	102.70
Repairs and service				
Parking		6.90		6.90
Car tax				
		94.30	15.30	109.60
OTHER TRAVEL COSTS				
(Specify) *Train (London)*		52.00		52.00
TELEPHONE EXPENSES				
(Attach telephone bill)				
OTHER				
(Entertaining, subsistence etc)		35.97	6.29	42.26
Dinner (2 nights)				
TOTAL CLAIMED		182.27	21.59	253.86

Signature of claimant: *C Prior*   Date: *29/5/X5*

Authorised by: *T Jones*   Date: *29 May 20X5*

Expenses claim form

Name: *James Clark* Month: *May*
Department: *Sales*

	Nominal ledger code	NET £	VAT £	TOTAL £
MOTOR CAR EXPENSES				
Petrol		117.42	20.55	137.97
Repairs and service				
Parking		14.50		14.50
Car tax				
		131.92	20.55	152.47
OTHER TRAVEL COSTS				
(Specify) *Taxi*		10.00		10.00
TELEPHONE EXPENSES				
(Attach telephone bill)		28.72	5.03	33.75
OTHER				
(Entertaining, subsistence etc)				
TOTAL CLAIMED		170.64	25.58	196.22

Signature of claimant: *J Clark* Date: *29 May 20X5*
Authorised by: *T Jones* Date: *29 May 20X5*

Sundry invoices received

Note. These invoices are *not* recorded in the purchase ledger.

Speedy Transport Ltd
42, Belman's Yard
Liverpool

Ives plc
Works Lane
Walsall

Vat no: 91844619
Date: 2205X5
Tax point: 2205X5
Invoice number: 174827
Your reference: TJ1723

TO:	PRICE	VAT	TOTAL
Delivery from your address to Peacock's Ltd 13, Brand Lane, Aberdeen VAT rate 17.5%	1,472.00	257.60	1,729.60
	1,472.00	257.60	1,729.60

Invoice

johnson's plastic products

302 Birbeck Estate
Birmingham

Ives plc
Works Lane
Walsall

Vat no: 116 428 32
Invoice number: 42767
Date:
Tax point: 20/5/X5
Your reference: R81617

	QTY	PRICE	TOTAL
10 gall pink dye	3	110.90	332.70
10 gall blue dye	2	110.90	221.80
10 gall yellow dye	1	110.90	110.90
			665.40
VAT at 17.5%			116.45
			781.85

DAWES STATIONERY

297 Hillside Road
Walsall
01922 472136

VAT no: 427 316 82

TO: Ives plc
Works Lane
Walsall

DATE: 28 May 20X5
TAX POINT: 28 May 20X5

INVOICE NO: 1728

	£
14 column analysis x 3	56.85
Petty cash book x 1	17.95
Petty cash voucher pads x 5	12.50
Hole punch x 2	11.20
Stapler x 1	4.45
	102.95
VAT at 17.5%	18.02
	120.97

```
                OFFICE SUPPLIES LTD
                     1 Blackstone Way
                          Walsall
                      01922 581 729
                    VAT no: 227 311 95

  To   Ives plc        Date    21/5/X5        Inv. No.    27131
       Works Lane
       Walsall         Tax point   21/5/X5

      Supply one typewriter                £
      Olympia 429XA                     425.00
          Ribbons                        21.75
                                        446.75
      VAT @ 17.5%                        78.18

                                        524.93
```

Mr Chester's new company car

The Chairman has decided that the prestige of the firm would be enhanced by the purchase of a Rolls Royce for his use. The car was ordered and it has now arrived at the garage and is waiting collection. The invoice shown below has been received and payment is to be by banker's draft.

PLUMY MOTORS Limited

4 POSH COURT
BIRMINGHAM

INVOICE 11719

Date: 29 May 20X5
Tax Point: 29 May 20X5
VAT No: 511 237 44

	Net	VAT	Total
ROLLS ROYCE Registration IVE 543P			
Basic price	61,275.00	10,723.13	71,998.13
Extras	452.14	—	452.14
	61,727.14	10,723.13	72,450.27

Practice devolved assessment (data and tasks)

Insurance charges for the next year

The following letter has been received by Ives plc from its insurers.

Flood and Fire Insurers
22 Markham Tower
Birmingham

Managing Director
Ives plc
Works Lane
Walsall

0121 492 4717

12 May 20X5

Our ref: FF/BJM/23

Dear Sir,

Insurance premiums 20X5/X6

The following premiums will apply for the year 18 May 20X5 to 17 May 20X6.

	£
Buildings insurance	4,278.42
Industrial accident insurance	1,894.87
Fidelity insurance	248.50
Machine insurance (schedule attached)	2,129.00
Car insurance (schedule attached)	3,821.76
Other contents insurance	1,467.65
Public liability cover	1,079.08
Legal cover surcharge	150.00
	15,069.28

We are happy to continue the current arrangement of payment over 12 months by standing order. Please instruct your bank to pay as follows.

Account name	Flood and Fire
Account number	4117329
Bank	Trustform
Sorting code	27-31-22
Address	Palmy Court Birmingham
Amount	£1,255.77

We would wish the first payment to take place at the date of commencement of the cover, or as close to that date as possible.

Should you wish to pay in some other way or if you have any queries, please do not hesitate to contact me.

Yours faithfully,

For FLOOD AND FIRE
J R Owen

Bank statements

Northern Bank				**CONFIDENTIAL**
17 Balsam Lane Birmingham BH 2SP Telephone 0121 493 7268 20X5		Account IVES plc Works Lane Walsall Statement date 3 June 20X5		SHEET NO 253 Account no 30595713

Date	Details	Withdrawals	Deposits	Balance (£)
29 May	Balance from Sheet no. 252			221,497.82
29 May	Bank charges	259.64		
	Bank interest	432.27		
	BACS salaries	55,327.92		
	Balance to Sheet no.254			165,477.99

Key   **SO** Standing Order   **DV** Dividend   **CC** Cash &/or Cheques   **AW** Auto withdrawals   **PY** Payroll   **Interest** - see over
       EC Eurocheque   **TR** Transfer   **CP** Card Purchases   **DD** Direct Debit   **OD** Overdrawn

Practice devolved assessment
3 Conway

Performance criteria

The following performance criteria are covered in this Devolved Assessment.

Element 2.1 Process documents relating to goods and services received

5   Entries are coded and recorded in the appropriate ledger

Element 2.2 Prepare authorised payments

2   Payments are scheduled and authorised by the appropriate person

3   Queries are referred to the appropriate person

4   Security and confidentiality are maintained according to organisational requirements

Element 2.3 Make and record payments

3   Payments are entered into accounting records according to organisational procedures

4   Queries are referred to the appropriate person

5   Security and confidentiality are maintained according to organisational requirements

Notes on completing the Assessment

This Assessment involves posting the entries to a cash book. The cash book is run both manually and on computer. Students with access to a computer can perform the Assessment using a computerised accounting package, although some modification of the question may be necessary. Students without access to a computer should post the cash book manually. The solution is given in both computerised and manual format.

You are allowed 2 hours to complete your work

A high level of accuracy is required. Check your work carefully.

Correcting fluid may be used but should be used in moderation. Errors should be crossed out neatly and clearly. You should write in black ink and not in pencil.

A full solution to this Assessment is provided on page 201 of this Kit.

Do not turn to the suggested solution until you have completed all parts of the Assessment.

Practice devolved assessment (data and tasks)

PRACTICE DEVOLVED ASSESSMENT 3: CONWAY

Data

Conway Ltd was incorporated five years ago. The company specialises in designing, stocking and developing gardens, usually those associated with large estates and houses. The company employs 30 people and the number of clients at any one time never exceeds six. The company uses only a dozen suppliers for garden materials, plants, trees and so on.

The company has expanded quite rapidly over the last few years and it has been decided that a computer would help to deal with stock control, salaries, the cash book and sundry other matters. The computer will be run in parallel with the manual system for three months as a check on the effectiveness and accuracy of the computer.

The low numbers of suppliers and customers mean that a complex accounting package is not considered necessary, particularly as customers change completely from year to year. The suppliers have been assigned individual codes in the main ledger, rather than in a separate purchase ledger. Invoices and credit notes are posted directly into these accounts and payments are recorded through the cash book. VAT is accounted for in the cash book for all payments *except for* the transactions with *suppliers* (who have individual accounts in the main ledger).

Most payments are by cheque unless otherwise stated.

Tasks

Using the information and documents on the following pages, complete the tasks outlined below for July 20X5.

(a) Using the computerised cash book, post all the payments shown for July, using the correct codes and extracting the VAT where necessary.

(b) Using the manual analysed cash book pages, post the transactions shown for July excluding the VAT where necessary.

(c) Balance off the cash book (whether computerised or manual) at the end of 31 July 20X5.

Note: VAT should be rounded up or down to the nearest penny.

Documents for use in the solution

Documents which are required in the solution are:

(a) example of computer screen for cash payments
(b) blank manual cash book pages (payments)

Computer screen

The following screen is an example of the type of information required in a computerised cash payments book.

System XX4 BANK PAYMENTS 31 July 20X5

N/C Name: BANK CURRENT ACCOUNT   Tax rate:
Batch Total:

N/C DEP	DATE	CHEQUE DETAILS	Net amount	Tax amount	Gross amount

Manual cash book: payments

						JULY - PAYMENTS
Date	Details	Cheque No	Total	VAT	Purchase Credit	Purchases Sundry

Heat & light	Bank charges interest	Telephone	Rates & water rates	Motor expenses	Print, post & stationery	Wages and salaries	Fixed Assets	Petty cash & Sundry

Practice devolved assessment (data and tasks)

Cash transactions in July 20X5

The cash transactions in July 20X5 and other relevant information is listed under the following headings.

(a) Balance brought forward
(b) Payments
(c) Main ledger codes
(d) Bank statements for July 20X5

Balance brought forward

The balance in the cash book at the end of 30 June 20X5 was £28,742.45 DR.

Payments: July 20X5

Date	Payee and details	Cheque No.	Amount paid £	VAT rate %
4.7.X5	Armin Specialist Plants	113724	335.71	17.5
4.7.X5	Elwin Garden Suppliers	113725	4,425.78	17.5
4.7.X5	New Forest Tree Nursery	113726	12,840.33	17.5
5.7.X5	Leaver Garden Tools	113727	3,056.36	17.5
5.7.X5	Moss and Blythe Nurseries	113728	650.00	17.5
11.7.X5	Wages: M Payne	113729	95.82	-
11.7.X5	Wages: W Bark	113730	95.82	-
11.7.X5	RIC Aggregates	113731	3,492.01	17.5
12.7.X5	Jackson & Brown Seeds	113732	839.29	17.5
12.7.X5	Mack's Garage: Motor Car	113733	21,567.45	-
12.7.X5	Chadwick Shrubs	113734	87.13	17.5
12.7.X5	Water Garden Specialists	113735	8,974.16	17.5
12.7.X5	Moss and Blythe Nurseries	113736	209.81	17.5
17.7.X5	Electricity Board	S/O	185.20	17.5
17.7.X5	Leaver Garden Tools	113737	1,248.59	17.5
17.7.X5	Robinson Nurseries	113738	5,697.05	17.5
17.7.X5	Armin Specialist Plants	113739	220.06	17.5
19.7.X5	Woodhouse Building Supplies	113740	2,097.97	17.5
19.7.X5	Cancelled	113741	-	17.5
19.7.X5	British Telecom	113742	120.47	17.5
25.7.X5	Leaver Garden Tools	113743	3,428.80	17.5
25.7.X5	Moss and Blythe Nurseries	113744	258.94	17.5
25.7.X5	RIC Aggregates	113745	6,082.88	17.5
26.7.X5	British Gas	113746	264.74	17.5
26.7.X5	Chadwick Shrubs	113747	194.47	17.5
30.7.X5	Bishop's Plant Hire	113748	8,309.90	17.5
30.7.X5	Rates	D/D	417.60	-
30.7.X5	Salaries	BACS	31,721.82	-
30.7.X5	Petty cash	113749	327.66	-

Main ledger codes

1000	Bank	5570	Salaries
1100	VAT	5590	Motor expenses
4110	Water Garden Specialists	5600	Travelling and entertainment
4120	Chadwick Shrubs	5610	Printing and stationery
4130	Bishop's Plant Hire	5620	Professional fees
4140	RIC Aggregates	5630	Depreciation
4150	New Forest Tree Nursery	5640	Bank charges and interest
4160	Moss and Blythe Nurseries	5650	Maintenance
4170	Elwin Garden Suppliers	5660	Bad debts
4180	Leaver Garden Tools	5670	General/sundry
4190	Robinson Nurseries	5900	Purchases
4200	Jackson and Brown Seed Merchants	6000	Petty cash
4210	Armin Specialist Plants	7210	Plant and machinery
4220	Woodhouse Buidling supplies	7220	Motor cars
5500	Insurance	7230	Freehold property
5510	Gas	7250	Stock
5520	Electricity	7260	Investments
5530	Rates (UBR)	7410	Sundry creditors
5540	Water rates	7420	Loans
5550	Telephone	7430	Share capital
5560	Casual labour	7440	Reserves

Summary

4100 - 4499	Supplier codes (creditors)
5500 - 5999	Expense/revenue codes
7200 - 7299	Asset codes
7400 - 7599	Liability codes

Practice devolved assessment (data and tasks)

Bank statements

Studio Bank   CONFIDENTIAL

5 High Street
Guildford
Surrey

Account: Conway Ltd
Hilltop Farm
Godalming
Surrey

SHEET NO 66

Telephone 01244 472318

20X5 Statement date 7 July 20X5 Account no 1443277

Date	Details		Withdrawals	Deposits	Balance (£)
1 July	Balance from sheet no.	65			20,646.85
2 July	Charges		448.21		
		113643	59.75		
		113710	158.05		
	CC			9,394.78	29,375.62
3 July	CC			7,960.88	37,336.50
5 July	CC			1,284.74	
		113721	456.25		
		113722	507.30		37,657.69
7 July	CC			8,619.03	
		113723	88.41		
		113726	12,840.33		33,347.98
7 July	Balance to Sheet no.	67			33,347.98

Key	SO Standing Order	DV Dividend	CC Cash &/or Cheques	AW Auto withdrawals	PY Payroll	Interest -see over
	EC Eurocheque	TR Transfer	CP Card Purchases	DD Direct Debit	OD Overdrawn	

Studio Bank — CONFIDENTIAL

5 High Street
Guildford
Surrey

Account: Conway Ltd
Hilltop Farm
Godalming
Surrey

SHEET NO 67

Telephone 01244 472318

20X5 Statement date 15 July 20X5 Account no 1443277

Date	Details		Withdrawals	Deposits	Balance (£)
7 July	Balance from sheet no.	66			33,347.98
8 July		113724	335.71		
		113725	4,425.78		
		113728	650.00		27,936.49
9 July		113727	3,056.36		24,880.13
13 July	CC			15,572.34	40,452.47
14 July		113729	95.82		
		113730	95.82		
		113729	95.82		40,165.01
15 July		113733	21,567.45		
		113735	8,974.16		9,623.40
15 July	Balance to Sheet no.	68			9,623.40

Key: **SO** Standing Order **DV** Dividend **CC** Cash &/or Cheques **AW** Auto withdrawals **PY** Payroll **Interest** -see over
EC Eurocheque **TR** Transfer **CP** Card Purchases **DD** Direct Debit **OD** Overdrawn

---

Studio Bank — CONFIDENTIAL

5 High Street
Guildford
Surrey

Account: Conway Ltd
Hilltop Farm
Godalming
Surrey

SHEET NO 68

Telephone 01244 472318

20X5 Statement date 23 July 20X5 Account no 1443277

Date	Details		Withdrawals	Deposits	Balance (£)
15 July	Balance from sheet no.	67			9,623.40
16 July	CC			2,007.08	
		113731	3,492.01		
		113732	839.29		7,212.05
		113734	87.13		7,026.85
17 July	SO		185.20		
20 July	SO Rebate			72.50	
		113738	5,697.05		
		113739	220.06		1,182.24
21 July	DD Water		332.29		849.95
22 July		113737	1,248.59		398.64 **OD**
23 July	CC			10,747.92	10,349.28
23 July	Balance to Sheet no.	69			10,349.28

Key: **SO** Standing Order **DV** Dividend **CC** Cash &/or Cheques **AW** Auto withdrawals **PY** Payroll **Interest** -see over
EC Eurocheque **TR** Transfer **CP** Card Purchases **DD** Direct Debit **OD** Overdrawn

Practice devolved assessment (data and tasks)

Studio Bank   CONFIDENTIAL

5 High Street
Guildford
Surrey

Account: Conway Ltd
Hilltop Farm
Godalming
Surrey

SHEET NO 69

Telephone 01244 472318

20X5   Statement date 31 July 20X5   Account no 1443277

Date	Details	Withdrawals	Deposits	Balance (£)
23 July	Balance from sheet no. 68			10,349.28
24 July	113742	120.47		10,228.81
27 July	Unauthorised OD Fee	150.00		
	CC		2,712.53	12,791.34
28 July	113742	120.47		
	CC		8,229.09	20,899.96
29 July	113744	258.94		20,641.02
30 July	BACS Salaries	31,721.82		
	DD Rates	417.60		11,498.40 **OD**
31 July	Balance to Sheet no. 70			11,498.40 **OD**

Key								
	SO Standing Order	DV Dividend	CC Cash &/or Cheques	AW Auto withdrawals	PY Payroll	**Interest** -see over
	EC Eurocheque	TR Transfer	CP Card Purchases	DD Direct Debit	OD Overdrawn	

Practice devolved assessment
4 Micawber

Performance criteria

The following performance criteria are covered in this Devolved Assessment.

Element 2.1 Process documents relating to goods and services received

5   Entries are coded and recorded in the appropriate ledger

6   Discrepancies are identified and either resolved or referred to the appropriate person if outside own authority

7   Communications with suppliers regarding accounts are handled politely and effectively

Element 2.3 Make and record payments

3   Payments are entered into accounting records according to organisational procedures

4   Queries are referred to the appropriate person

5   Security and confidentiality are maintained according to organisational requirements

Notes on completing the Assessment

This Assessment is designed to test your ability to post transactions correctly to the ledger accounts and deal with other matters concerned with credit purchases.

You are provided with data under each of parts (a) to (b) necessary to perform the related tasks.

You are allowed 2 hours to complete your work

A high level of accuracy is required. Check your work carefully.

Correcting fluid may be used but should be used in moderation. Errors should be crossed out neatly and clearly. You should write in black ink and not in pencil.

A full suggested solution to this Assessment is provided on page 205 of this Kit.

Do not turn to the suggested solution until you have completed all parts of the Assessment.

PRACTICE DEVOLVED ASSESSMENT 4: MICAWBER

Data

You are employed as an Accounting Technician by Micawber Holdings Ltd ('Micawber'), and you are involved in purchase ledger work.

Micawber's accounting system is non-integrated, meaning that the main ledger module is separate from the purchase ledger and normal invoice processing. Summary totals and journal adjustments are posted in two separate operations.

(a) It is now 11 June 20X5, and you have been given the following.

  (1) Two memos from your boss

  (2) A letter from a supplier who is also a customer

  (3) A purchase day book batch 6/04, for posting on 11 June

  (4) The day's entries from the purchase returns book (batch R6/1)

  (5) A cheque listing produced by the purchase ledger system to pay outstanding balances at 30 April 20X5 (unless otherwise instructed)

  (6) Details extracted from a manual cheque book

  (7) Purchase ledger accounts

For the sake of audit trail, each transaction has a reference.

  (1) The transaction reference for invoices is given in purchase day book batches.

  (2) The transaction reference for computer cheques is the cheque number on the listing.

  (3) The transaction reference for the credit notes received etc is given in purchase returns day book batches.

  (4) For all other items (for example manual cheques) the transaction reference is the journal number.

  (5) The double entry is carried out on a daily summary basis. A journal is raised for double entry items.

  There are two types of adjustment.

  - *Memorandum account adjustments* alter accounts (eg purchase ledger) that do *not* form party of the double entry.

  - *Main account journals* are double entry items.

4: Micawber

Tasks

Using the information provided:

(i) post the computer generated items to the individual creditor accounts.

(ii) draw up the journal entries, distinguishing clearly between memorandum account adjustments and nominal account journals, and post them to the ledger accounts.

Note. You do not need to produce the memorandum journals in part (ii) for the computer generated items in part (i).

VAT should be rounded up or down to the nearest penny.

1st memo

To: Accounting Technician
From: Y Ourboss, Chief Accountant
Date: 10/6/X5

Re: CRITCHLEY PLC

The litigation about our debt to them of £15,071.93 has finally been concluded. We are to pay them a lump sum of £8,000, and they will cancel the rest of the debt.

Please draw up and put through the relevant journals, and close down the account.

2nd memo

To: Accounting Technician
From: Y Ourboss, Chief Accountant
Date: 10/6/X5

Pickwick are pressing us for payment of an invoice for £190.05. I can't find it on the ledger.

However, I have discovered it was misposted to Nell's account - please adjust (Trans Ref is 4712 and it was posted 23/4/X5 and has also been paid).

Please take necessary steps and draw up a journal, and put it through.

Letter from supplier who is also a customer

Dorrit
Weston Industrial Estate
Liverpool
4 June 20X5

Att Purchase Ledger
Micawber Holdings
Blazing Row
Skulduggery
Merseyside

Dear Sir

As part of our end of month procedures we wish to contra our sales ledger and purchase ledger balance of 31/5/20X5 of £17,051.61 with yourselves.

We propose that our purchase ledger balance of 31/5/20X5 of £17,051.61 with yourselves be reduced by our sales ledger balance with yourselves of £4,509.90 at 31 May 20X5.

Please confirm that this arrangement is acceptable to you. As far as we are aware, none of the invoices or transactions giving rise to these balances are in dispute.

Yours faithfully,

R Hughes
Financial Controller

Please action
Y Ourboss

Practice devolved assessments (data and tasks)

Purchase day book batch 6/04

11/6/X5 Our Ref	Acc		Invoice total £ p	VAT £ p	Net £ p
6210	131	Scrooge	72.90	10.86	62.04
6211	89	Dorrit	85.29	12.70	72.59
6212	105	Pickwick	581.63	86.63	495.00
6213	131	Scrooge	11,422.61	1,701.24	9,721.37
6214	104	Pip	257.87	38.41	219.46
6215	121	Rudge	1,152.83	171.70	981.13
6216	87	Copperfield	737.02	109.77	627.25
6217	113	Nell	6,116.91	911.03	5,205.88
TOTAL			20,427.06	3,042.34	17,384.72

Purchase returns day book batch R6/1

11/6/X5 Our Ref	Acc		Invoice total £ p	VAT £ p	Net £ p
CN493	105	Pickwick	500.00	74.47	425.53

Cheque list C6/1 - 11 June 20X5

Account	Name	Cheque no	£ p
131	Scrooge	100859	5,312.20
87	Copperfield	100860	834.91
121	Rudge	100861	366.66
104	Pip	100862	545.30
113	Nell	100863	951.25
			8,010.32

Manual cheques

11/6/X5	Critchley plc	Cheque 70912	£8,000

Purchase ledger accounts

SUPPLIER: COPPERFIELD   ACCOUNT NO: 87

Date	Batch/narrative	Trans Ref	£ (DR)/CR	£ Balance
1/6/X5	Balance b/d			991.99
3/6/X5	6/01	6032	792.11	1,784.10
5/6/X5	6/02	6055	175.60	1,959.70
9/6/X5	6/03	6178	264.47	2,224.17

SUPPLIER: RUDGE   ACCOUNT NO: 121

Date	Batch/narrative	Trans Ref	£ (DR)/CR	£ Balance
1/6/X5	Balance b/d			876.40

SUPPLIER: PIP				ACCOUNT NO: 104
Date	Batch/narrative	Trans Ref	£ (DR)/CR	£ Balance
1/6/X5	Balance b/d			655.30
9/6/X5	6/03	6190	843.00	1,498.30

SUPPLIER: CRITCHLEY PLC				ACCOUNT NO: 42
Date	Batch/narrative	Trans Ref	£ (DR)/CR	£ Balance
1/6/X5	Balance b/d			15,071.93

SUPPLIER: DORRIT				ACCOUNT NO: 89
Date	Batch/narrative	Trans Ref	£ (DR)/CR	£ Balance
1/6/X5	Balance b/d			4,509.90
3/6/X5	6/01	6001	410.11	4,920.01
5/6/X5	6/02	6053	973.75	5,893.76

SUPPLIER: NELL				ACCOUNT NO: 113
Date	Batch/narrative	Trans Ref	£ (DR)/CR	£ Balance
1/6/X5	Balance b/d			1,917.11
3/6/X5	6/01	6042	231.90	2,149.01
9/6/X5	6/03	6012	8.52	2,157.53
9/6/X5	R6/1	C/N 492	(20.20)	2,137.33

SUPPLIER: SCROOGE				ACCOUNT NO: 131
Date	Batch/narrative	Trans Ref	£ (DR)/CR	£ Balance
1/6/X5	Balance b/d			7,759.50

SUPPLIER: PICKWICK				ACCOUNT NO: 105
Date	Batch/narrative	Trans Ref	£ (DR)/CR	£ Balance
1/6/X5	Balance b/d			80.12

Practice devolved assessments (data and tasks)

(b) **Data**

Micawber has its business bank account with the Lancashire Bank. Whenever Micawber goes overdrawn, it pays interest of 1.5% per month of the amount overdrawn. It earns no interest on a credit balance.

One of Micawber's suppliers, Copperfield, offers discounts for early settlement of its invoices.

From their statement at 31 August 20X5, you owed Copperfield £10,000. They will give a 1% discount if you settle within a month. You would generally expect to pay after 2 months if there was no financial incentive to pay early (ie a further 30 days later).

Your firm's procedures manual states that 'advantage shall be taken of settlement discounts if it is of financial benefit to the company'.

Task

Address the following question.

Should you take advantage of Copperfield's offer, assuming there are no other liabilities, if your current bank balance is:

(i) £5,000 (in your favour)?
(ii) nil?

(*Hint*. Calculate the amount of the discount and compare it with the interest you would be charged by the bank if you paid early.)

Practice devolved assessment
5 Needham Baddely

Performance criteria

The following performance criteria are covered in this Devolved Assessment.

Element 2.1 Process documents relating to goods and services received

1. Suppliers' invoices and credit notes are checked against delivery notes, ordering documentation and evidence that goods or services have been received
2. Totals and balances are correctly calculated and checked on suppliers' invoices
3. Available discounts are identified and deducted
4. Documents are correctly entered as primary records according to organisational procedures
5. Entries are coded and recorded in the appropriate ledger
6. Discrepancies are identified and either resolved or referred to the appropriate person if outside own authority
7. Communications with suppliers regarding accounts are handled politely and effeciently

Notes on completing the Assessment

This Assessment is designed to test your ability to process purchase orders and documentation from suppliers.

You are provided with data under each of parts (a) to (d) necessary to perform the related tasks.

You are allowed 3 hours to complete your work

A high level of accuracy is required. Check your work carefully.

Correcting fluid may be used but should be used in moderation. Errors should be crossed out neatly and clearly. You should write in black ink and not in pencil.

A full solution to this Assessment is provided on page 209 of this Kit.

Do not turn to the suggested solution until you have completed all parts of the Assessment.

Practice devolved assessments (data and tasks)

PRACTICE DEVOLVED ASSESSMENT 5: NEEDHAM BADDELY

Data

You work as a purchase ledger clerk for Needham Baddely Ltd. The following is an extract from a price list supplied to you by W E Gotham Components plc, a company you deal with regularly.

W E GOTHAM COMPONENTS - PRICE LIST			
Product	Product ref		£ p
Grade 1 widget 2cm × 12cm	XLS	24	123 45
Grade 1 widget 1 cm × 12cm	XLS	12	92 58
Triple-spoked ratchet 3cm × 6cm	TSR	18	67 89
Magnetised sprocket 2cm × 9cm	WMS	18	90 12
Circuit extender link 25	CXL	25	154 31
Positive link extender 125	PLX	125	317 89
Positive link extender 200	PLX	200	508 62
Tension-poled reactor 600	TPR	600	217 98
Deep image manipulator: effects	DIM	FX2	72 66
Particle accelerator (CERN compatible)	CER	870	1,499 99
Myco-Simulator 9-phase	MYS	EO9	765 95
Myco-Simulator single-phase	MYS	EO1	675 05
Energised Reduced-Feedback Distributor	ERF	010	51 86
Quark Humidifying Sink	HEW	051	207 44
Sonic Orgone Negater	SON	959	115 95
Kinetic Anti-reactor 959 Hz	KAR	210	416 43
Neologism Controller (Ergonomic)	ENC	119	115 55
Rhomboid Oscillating Widget	ROW	510	370 35
Low-energy Tardis motor	LEY	666	53 97
Ultra-low energy Tardis motor	VET	999	107 94

Note. VAT at 17½% is charged on all the above products. VAT is *not* included in the prices quoted above. VAT should be rounded down to the nearest penny.

The following facts are relevant.

(1) You are a trade customer. Your agreement with W E Gotham plc is that you get a 3% discount on the first £2,000 worth of goods *per order*, and a 6% discount thereafter. The 3% and 6% discounts are calculated *after* any other special offers have been allowed for, but *before* VAT.

(2) On 1 September 20X5 you received through the post the following advertisement from W E Gotham Components plc, detailing some special offers.

YOU WANT 'EM?

LOOK NO FURTHER!

WE GOTHAM COMPONENTS PLC

For September, and September only, 'we got' these unbeatable, unrepeatable deals for trade customers!

SAVE 25% on List price of 9-phase Myco-simulators!!!!!

SAVE 20% on Positive Link Extenders 200!!!!!!

Buy TWO Ultra-Low energy Tardis motors and get a low energy tardis motor **free** (if requested).

HURRY WHILE STOCKS LAST

GO GET 'EM AT GOTHAM!!

Practice devolved assessments (data and tasks)

(3) You have received the following memorandum from the stock controller.

MEMO

TO: A. Clerk, Purchases Ledger

FROM: O.B. Solete, Stock controller

DATE: 3/9/X5

PLEASE ORDER		NO. REQUIRED
• Grade 1 Widgets	2 x 12	4
	1 x 12	2
• Magnetised sprocket		1
• Particle accelerator		1
• Neologism controller (ergonomic)		5
• Ultra-low energy Tardis motor		4
• Low energy Tardis motor		2
• Myco-simulator single phase		9
• Positive link extenders 200		4

Please order A.S.A.P. delivery to Milkington Warehouse except Particle accelerator to Cambridge

---

(4) Your company has three warehouses.

- Dairy Street
  Milkington
  W Midlands WV5

- First Court St
  Cambridge CB2

- Druid St
  New Stonehenge
  Glastonbury

(5) The address of W E Gotham Components plc is:
Old Iron Gate Street
Wraillings Industrial Estate
Melchett

Tasks

(a) Complete the purchase order form. Attach workings to the purchase order you send to justify the level of discounts and allowances you hope to claim. Reference the purchase order to your workings. Note that it is Needham Baddely's policy:

(i) to calculate the price of each item before VAT at list price and to include it on the purchase order form (even if there is a special offer or discount available).

(ii) to treat special offers as if they were discounts in cases such as this.

So, fill in the list price by each item you require, and at the bottom of the form where it says 'discounts and special offers' note the total value of discounts and the special offers you hope to receive.

FROM: **NEEDHAM BADDELY LTD** PURCHASE ORDER NO: *901*
Skid Row
Wantage, OX22 TPN

TO: DATE:

VAT REG: *6 721 3941*

Please supply the following.

Your product reference	Item	Quantity	Your list price	Total (exc VAT)
			£ p	£ p

Total
Discounts and special offers
Net

Comments

(b) **Data**

It is now 1 October 20X5 and since the beginning of September you have received two invoices from W E Gotham Components plc. Also attached are a number of Goods Received Notes (GRNs) issued by your warehouses. (Your Purchase Order 901 was acknowledged on 4 September 20X5.)

Practice devolved assessments (data and tasks)

Tasks

(i) Check that the invoices are correct. Goods received notes are provided to help you. Note down any discrepancies; have you been billed for an amount that differs from your estimate on Purchase Order 901?

(ii) Explain what action you would take to deal with any discrepancies you find.

' GO GET 'EM AT GOTHAM!!'

W.E. GOTHAM COMPONENTS PLC

Old Iron Gate Street, Wraillings Industrial Estate, Melchett

SALES INVOICE

No: 7072   **Date/Tax point:** 6 September 20X5

Item	Your Order	List Price £ p	Total £ p
4 x XLS 24 Grade 1 (2 x 12) Widget	901	123 . 45	493 . 80
2 x XLS 12 Grade 1 (1 x 12) Widget	901	92 . 58	185 . 16
1 x WMS 18 Magnetised Sprocket	901	90 . 12	90 . 12
5 x ENC 119 Neologism Controller	901	115 . 55	577 . 75
4 x VET 999 Ultra-low Tardis Motor	901	107 . 94	431 . 76
2 x LEY 666 Low-energy Tardis Motor	901	53 . 97	107 . 94
9 x MYS EDI Single-phase Myco Simulator	901	675 . 05	6,075 . 45
4 x PLX 200 Positive Link Extender	901	508 . 62	2,034 . 48
TOTAL			9,996 . 46
DISCOUNTS			539 . 79
			9,456 . 67
VAT @ 17.5%			1,654 . 91
DUE			11,111 . 58

To: Attn Purchase Ledger
       Needham Baddely Ltd
       Skid Row
       Wantage

Reg Office: Old Iron Gate Street, Wraillings Industrial Estate, Melchett
Reg No: 82912
VAT Reg No: 5 439 832

'GO GET 'EM AT GOTHAM!!'

WE GOTHAM COMPONENTS PLC

Old Iron Gate Street, Wraillings Industrial Estate, Melchett

SALES INVOICE

No: 7074 **Date/Tax point:** 7 September 20X5

Item	Your Order	List Price £ p	Total £ p
1 x CER 870 Particle Accelerator (CERN)	901	1,499 . 99	1,499 . 99
TOTAL			1,499 . 99
DISCOUNTS			45 . 00
			1,454 . 99
VAT @ 17.5%			254 . 62
DUE			1,709 . 61

To: Attn Purchase Ledger
Needham Baddely Ltd
Skid Row
Wantage

Reg Office: Old Iron Gate Street, Wraillings Industrial Estate, Melchett
Reg No: 82912
VAT Reg No: 5 439 832

NEEDHAM BADDELY

GOODS RECEIVED NOTE

Site: Cambridge
Date: 7 September 20X5

No: C973

Item	Code	Quantity	Purchase Order No
CER 870 Particle Accelerator	4911	1	901

NEEDHAM BADDELY

GOODS RECEIVED NOTE

Site: Milkington
Date: 6 September 20X5

No: M9912

Item	Code	Quantity	Purchase Order No
ENC 119 Neologism Controller	9408	5	901
Single Phase Myco-Simulator	8397	9	901
Widgets (Grade 1) 2 x 12	7286	4	901
1 x 12	6175	2	901

NEEDHAM BADDELY

GOODS RECEIVED NOTE

Site: **Milkington** No: **M9914**

Date: **7 September 20X5**

Item	Code	Quantity	Purchase Order No
Magnetised sprocket WMS 18	3842	1	901
PLX 200 Positive Link Extender	2731	4	901
Ultra-low energy Tardis Motor VET 999	1620	4	901
Low energy Tardis Motor LEY 666	0519	4	901

(c) **Task**

Identify as many mistakes as you can on the GRN below, received from your Glastonbury warehouse. To help you, Needham Baddely Ltd's own list of stock codes is provided.

NEEDHAM BADDELY

GOODS RECEIVED NOTE

Site: Glastonbury No:

Date: October 20X5

Item	Code	Quantity	Purchase Order No
Circuit extender link 25	CXL25	4	931
Particle accelerator - TORUS	6911	1	940
7-phase myco-simulator	7519		920
Rhomboid oscillating widget	5655	1	896
Anoid oscillating widget	6565	7	896
Phenomenology inhibitor	1001	3	896
Magnetised sprocket	3842	1	941
Circuit training pump	9810	9	637
Particle accelerator - CERN	5911	4	
Sonic orgone negater	0825	6	639

NEEDHAM BADDELY STOCK CODES

Product	Stock code
Biostatic granules	2241
Ferrous salt	2014
Kryptonite nuggets	2102
Grade 1 Widget 2cm × 12cm	7286
Grade 1 Widget 1cm × 12cm	6175
Triple-spoked ratchet 3cm × 6cm	5064
Magnetised sprocket 2cm × 9cm	3842
Circuit extender link 25	4731
Circuit training pump	8910
Positive link extender 125	3620
Positive link extender 200	2731
Tension-poled reactor 600	7953
Deep image manipulator: effects	5731
Particle accelerator (CERN compatible)	4911
Particle accelerator (TORUS compatible)	5911
Myco-Simulator 9-phase	9519
Myco-Simulator 7-phase	7519
Myco-Simulator - single phase	1519
Energised Reduced-Feedback Distributor	1397
Quark Humidifying Sink	9173
Sonic Orgone Negater	0825
Kinetic Anti-reactor 959 Hz	1926
Neologism Controller (Ergonomic)	9408
Rhomboid Oscillating Widget	5655
Anoid Oscillating Widget	6655
Low-energy Tardis motor	0519
Ultra-low energy Tardis motor	1620
Phenomenology Inhibitor - 100 volts	1001

(d) *Data*

Isaac Faraday, the Finance Director of another supplier, Ergonome Ltd, has sent you a letter dated 2 October 20X5 demanding immediate payment of £5,227.10 to settle your account, and threatening recourse to solicitors.

The Chief Accountant, Lucas Legg, was not aware there was any problem with that account, so has asked you to investigate.

To do so, you assemble the following documentation.

(1) The statement sent to you by Ergonome Ltd
(2) A printout of the purchases ledger account you have with Ergonome Ltd
(3) Some invoices
(4) A number of Goods Received Notes
(5) Details from your cash book cheque listing
(6) A debit note

Tasks

(i) Reconcile the balance per Ergonome Ltd to your own records, analysing any discrepancies.

(ii) Explain what action you will now take to deal with Ergonome Ltd's letter.

(iii) Draft a letter to Ergonome Ltd for your boss to sign, explaining what you think the problems are and how you should sort them out.

ERGONOME LTD

(VAT Reg: 3 495 0721)

1 October 20X5

STATEMENT OF ACCOUNT

To Needham Baddely
    Skid Row
    Wantage
    OX22 7PN

Date			Amount £ p	Balance £ p
23/5/X5	Invoice	8379	1,060 . 71	1,060 . 71
24/7/X5	Invoice	8742	2,937 . 50	3,998 . 21
24/7/X5	Invoice	8743	2,350 . 00	6,348 . 21
24/9/X5	Invoice	8912	253 . 90	6,602 . 11
25/9/X5	Payment - thank you		1,375 . 01	5,227 . 10
	BALANCE AT 30/9/X5			5,227 . 10

Please send your remittance by return of post

OVERDUE BALANCE	5,227.10

REMINDER

Fonda House, 12 Angrimen Street, Pleading, LINCS (Reg office)   Phone: 01792 911324

5: Needham Baddely

Needham Baddely Ltd purchase ledger extract

Account Code: E41
Account Name: Ergonome Ltd
Supplier Address: Fonda House, 12 Angrimen Street, Pleading, Lincs
Status: Live
Date: 30 September 20X5

Date	Ref	Type	CR/DR - £	p	Balance £	p
24/7/X5	4397	Invoice 8742 - GRN G1724-5	2,937	50	2,937	50
3/8/X5	901	Debit Note 901	-1,562	49	1,375	01
24/9/X5		Invoice 8912 - GRN G2824	253	90	1,628	91
23/9/X5	490745	CHQ	-1,375	01	253	90
30/9/X5		BALANCE			253	90

Note. This extract shows all transactions entered to the purchase ledger system since 1 May 20X5.

Practice devolved assessments (data and tasks)

ERGONOME LTD
SALES INVOICE

Fonda House, 12 Angrimen Street
Pleading, Lincs

TO: Needham Baddely Ltd
        Skid Row
        Wantage OX22 7PN

F.A.O.:   Purchase Ledger

Invoice No:	8742
Account No:	NEE 2
Date/Tax Pt:	24/7/X5

	Quantity	Price £ p
Kryptonite Nuggets @ £20/kg - delivered 24/7/X5 Delivery note X121	100kg	2,000 . 00
Biostatic Granules @ £5 per tonne - delivered 24/7/X5 Delivery note X122	100 tonnes	500 . 00
		2,500 . 00
VAT at 17.5%		437 . 50
		2,937 . 50

VAT Reg: 3 495 0721

ERGONOME LTD
SALES INVOICE

Fonda House, 12 Angrimen Street
Pleading, Lincs

TO: D.E. Fences Ltd
        Chancery Court Yard
        Dock Green, Tugney

F.A.O.:   Purchase Ledger

Invoice No:	8743
Account No:	NEE 2
Date/Tax Pt:	24/7/X5

	Quantity	Price £ p
Kryptonite Nuggets @ £20/kg - delivered 24/7/X5 Delivery note X121	100kg	2,000 . 00
		2,000 . 00
VAT at 17.5%		350 . 00
		2,350 . 00

Please investigate
Check GRN a1724 & Invoice 8742
DON'T PROCESS
L Legg

VAT Reg: 3 495 0721

ERGONOME LTD — DUPLICATE INVOICE

Fonda House, 12 Angrimen Street
Pleading, Lincs

TO: Needham Baddely Ltd
Skid Row
Wantage OX22 7PN

F.A.O.: Purchase Ledger

Invoice No: 8379D
Account No: NEE2
Date/Tax Pt: 23/5/95
Duplicate Date: 1/10/X5

	Quantity	Price £ p
Biostatic Granules @ £5 per tonne Delivery note ref W055	170 tonnes	850 . 00
Ferrous salt @ £5.86/kg Delivery note ref W055	9kg	52 . 74
		902 . 74
VAT at 17.5%		157 . 97
		1,060 . 71

Check GRNs for Ergonome Ltd's delivery note ref
L Legg

VAT Reg: 3 495 0721

Note. This duplicate was received on 2 October 20X5.

NEEDHAM BADDELY
GOODS RECEIVED NOTE

Site: Glastonbury   No: G1672
Date: 23 May 20X5

Item	Code	Quantity	Purchase Order No
Biostatic Granules (Delivery note W055)	2241	170 tonnes	621
Ferrous salt (Delivery note W055)	2014	9 kg	621

NEEDHAM BADDELY

GOODS RECEIVED NOTE

Site: Glastonbury   No: G1724

Date: 24 July 20X5

Item	Code	Quantity	Purchase Order No
Kryptonite Nuggets (Delivery note X121)	2102	100 kg	723

NEEDHAM BADDELY

GOODS RECEIVED NOTE

Site: Glastonbury   No: G1725

Date: 24 July 20X5

Item	Code	Quantity	Purchase Order No
Biostatic Granules (Delivery note X122)	2241	100 tonnes	723

Cheque list extracts

Date	Account Name	Account No	Cheque No	£ p
23/9/X5	Zola	Z29	490741	624.11
	Dreyfuss	D12	490742	821.13
	Whistler	W92	490743	1,018.49
	Blewer	B10	490744	696.95
	Ergonome	E41	490745	1,375.01
	Clemence	C02	490746	53.07
	Plus Pipes	PP25	490747	409.48
	Olduvai	D81	490748	765.89

Date	Account Name	Account No	Cheque No	£	p
1/10/X5	Lee Poh	LP71	490749	511	19
	Ngugi	N32	490750	471	31
	Negretti	N21	490751	880	79
	O'Leary	OL2	490752	452	71
	Ann Chovy	AC1	490753	1,149	66
	Phil Chard	PC9	490754	827	72
	Radetzky	R17	490755	1,237	20
	Egonome	E41	490756	253	90

NEEDHAM BADDELY LTD
DEBIT NOTE

Number 901
Date 3/8/20X5

Narrative	£	p
65.956 tonnes of Biostatic Granules were faulty and could not be used.	329	78
50 kg of Kryptonite nuggets were defective.	1,000	00
Subtotal	1,329	78
VAT (17.5%)	232	71
TOTAL	1,562	49

We have debited our records accordingly.
Please credit yours.
Your REF: billed on invoice 8742

Skid Row, Wantage, OX22 7PN

86

Trial run devolved assessments

TRIAL RUN DEVOLVED ASSESSMENT 1
BARKERS

FOUNDATION STAGE - NVQ/SVQ2

Unit 2

Making and Recording Payments

The purpose of this Trial Run Devolved Assessment is to give you an idea of what an AAT simulation looks like. It is not intended as a definitive guide to the tasks you may be required to perform.

The suggested time allowance for this Assessment is **three hours**. Up to 30 minutes extra time may be permitted in an AAT simulation. Breaks in assessment will be allowed in the AAT simulation, but it must normally be completed in one day.

Calculators may be used but no reference material is permitted.

DO NOT OPEN THIS PAPER UNTIL YOU ARE READY TO START UNDER TIMED CONDITIONS

Trial run devolved assessments

INSTRUCTIONS

This Assessment is designed to test your ability to record and account for cash transactions.

The situation is provided on Page 91.

The tasks you are to perform are set out on Page 92.

You are provided with data on Pages 93 to 98 which you must use to complete the tasks.

Your answers should be set out in the answer booklet on Pages 99 to 114 using the documents provided. You may require additional answer pages.

You are allowed three hours to complete your work.

A high level of accuracy is required. Check your work carefully.

Correcting fluid may be used but should be used in moderation. Errors should be crossed out neatly and clearly. You should write in black ink, not pencil.

You are advised to read the whole of the Assessment before commencing as all of the information may be of value and is not necessarily supplied in the sequence in which you might wish to deal with it.

A full suggested solution to this Assessment is provided on Page 217 of this Kit.

THE SITUATION

Barkers Ltd was set up about ten years ago by George 'Bulldog' Barker to manufacture and sell dog kennels to both trade and retail customers.

There is a small shop/office attached to the company's factory in Dalmatian Road, Wagford. Barker's extensive range of kennels is on display in the shop and retail customers are welcome to browse and buy.

'Bulldog' Barker still owns and manages the company. As well as the four men who work in the factory, there are seven other members of staff. The finance director, Mr Bone, oversees the work of the bookkeeper/shop assistant, Lassie McDonald and you, Rex Cash, the accounts clerk. Mr Marrow, the sales director, has one sales person, Winifred Anne Lot, working for her. (Winifred prefers to be called Win.) Pat Pant, the purchasing clerk, reports to Mrs Growler, the purchases director.

Suppliers' statements are received towards the end of each month. It is company policy to pay suppliers at the end of the month only, taking advantage of any discounts available at that time.

Sundry invoices are also paid at the end of the month.

The management team can authorise expenditure to the limits shown below.

	Authorisation limit £
Mr B Barker	No limit
Mr T Bone	300
Mr A Marrow	200
Mrs B Growler	500

Cheques can only be prepared from authorised supporting documentation. Cheques must be signed by two directors, one director being Mr Barker if the amount is greater than £250.

Petty cash is maintained on an imprest system with a float of £100 replenished monthly. Lassie can make payments of up to £50. She can authorise expenditure of up to £20 herself. Expenditure from between £20 and £50 must be authorised by Mr Bone. Each petty cash voucher, once completed by Lassie, must be signed by the claimant and authorised by the relevant person.

Lassie runs a manual cash book to which she posts payments at the end of each month. She is also responsible for petty cash.

The company is registered for VAT. All purchases are standard rated unless stated otherwise.

Lassie has taken a holiday to the Isle of Skye and so you have been asked to carry out the month-end procedures. She has delegated to you her responsibilities and powers, for example, authorisation.

Trial run devolved assessments

THE TASKS TO BE PERFORMED

In the answer booklet on Pages 99 to 114 complete the tasks outlined below for April 20X5 month-end procedures. Data for this assessment is provided on Pages 93 to 98.

1. Examine the suppliers' statements. On the basis of the instructions shown, prepare remittance advices. (*Note*. Credit notes should be offset aginst most recent preceding invoices for the calculation of discounts, unless stated otherwise.)

2. Obtain authorisation for payment of the trade suppliers' invoices.

3. Examine the expense claim. State what documentation you would require to support the claim. State which manager could authorise the claim.

4. Prepare a cheque requisition for the expense claim.

5. Obtain approval for payment of the stationery invoice. (Note that this invoice is to be paid straight away and not recorded in the purchase ledger.)

6. Complete the bank giro credit payment slip for the payment to Dirty Water for water rates.

7. Prepare cheques for the payments in 1, 4, 5 and 6. Cross cheques for suppliers 'Not Negotiable'.

8. Prepare the payments side of the cash book for April.

9. Using the petty cash information on Pages 97 to 98, carry out the following tasks.

    (a) Where appropriate prepare petty cash vouchers for the receipts and claims made by members of staff. Where it would not be appropriate to prepare a petty cash voucher state what alternative procedure might be followed.

    (b) Arrange the vouchers in date order and number each one. (The last voucher in March 20X5 was 152.)

    (c) Enter the voucher details into the petty cash book on Page 109.

    (d) Total and balance off the petty cash book for the month ended 30 April 20X5, including the entries necessary to top up the imprest amount. (Note that, because petty cash was running low at the end of the month, a cheque (no 101100) has already been cashed for this amount before writing up the petty cash book.)

    (e) Transfer the totals of the analysis columns of the petty cash book to the main ledger accounts on Pages 110 to 112.

10. Using the information on the bank statement, make any necessary additional postings to the cash book. The petty cash top up should also be shown.

11. Balance off the cash book and post the totals to the main ledger accounts on Pages 110 to 112. Balance off the ledger accounts and carry forward balances.

Note: VAT should be rounded up or down to the nearest penny.

1: Barkers (data and tasks)

DATA

(a) The following suppliers' statements were received at the end of April.

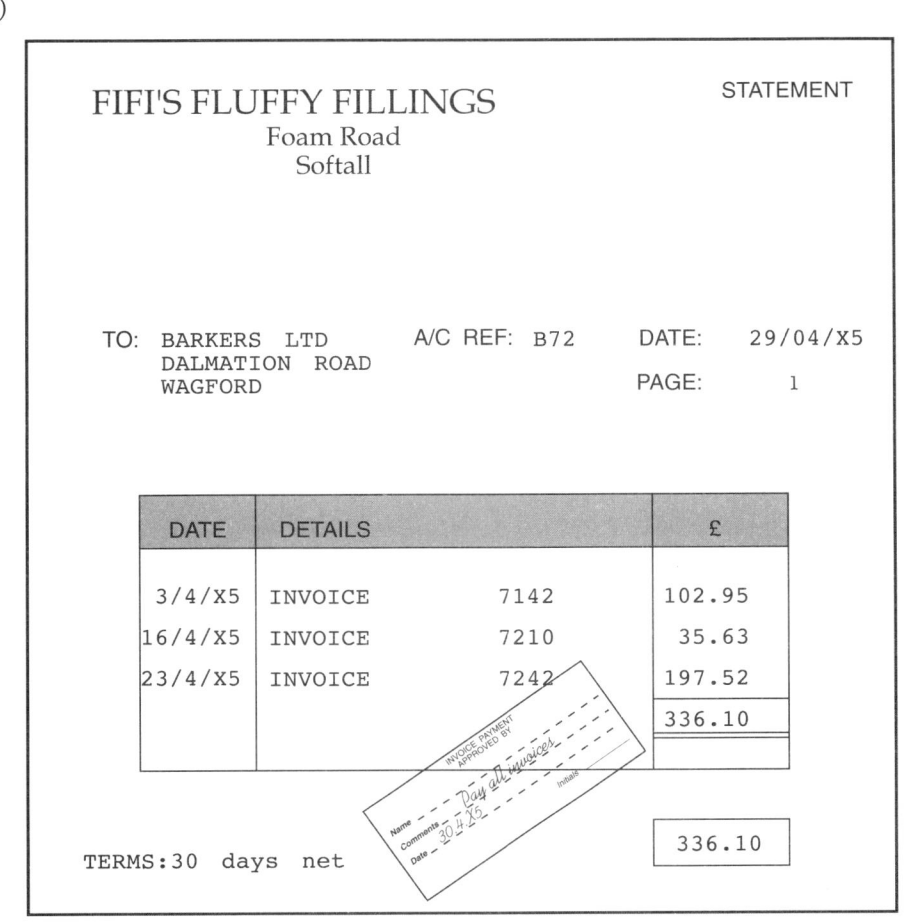

(i)

FIFI'S FLUFFY FILLINGS
Foam Road
Softall

STATEMENT

TO: BARKERS LTD
DALMATION ROAD
WAGFORD

A/C REF: B72

DATE: 29/04/X5
PAGE: 1

DATE	DETAILS		£
3/4/X5	INVOICE	7142	102.95
16/4/X5	INVOICE	7210	35.63
23/4/X5	INVOICE	7242	197.52
			336.10

INVOICE PAYMENT APPROVED BY
Name _____
Comments: Pay all invoices
Date: 30.4.X5
Initials _____

336.10

TERMS: 30 days net

Trial run devolved assessments

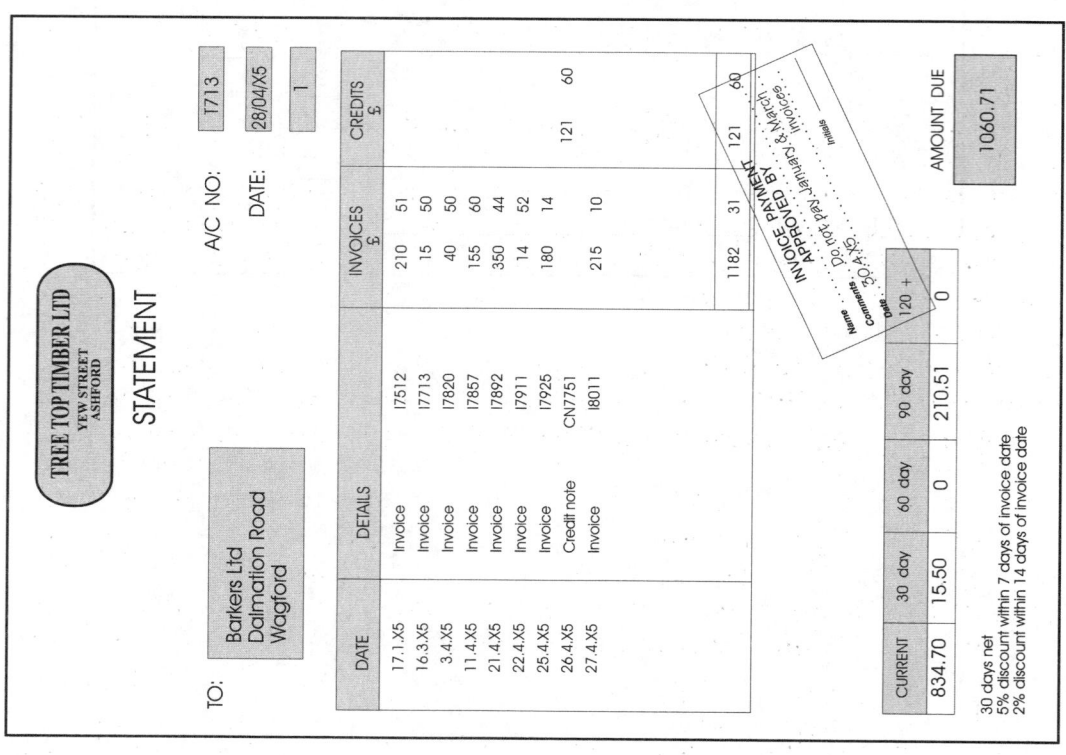

(iii)

Nick's Nails
Hammer Road
Bangington

STATEMENT

DATE: 29/4/X5

A/C REF: B11510

PAGE: 1

TO: Barkers Ltd
Dalmation Road
Wagford

DATE	DETAILS	INVOICES		CREDITS	
1.4.X5	Invoice N7252	40	22		
7.4.X5	Invoice N7263	21	50		
19.4.X5	Invoice N7292	14	90		
21.4.X5	C/Note CN7210			11	50
28.4.X5	Invoice N7321	11	50		
		88	12	11	50

Terms: 30 days net
8.5% discount for payment
within 14 days of invoice date

Invoice payment approved by ...... Pay all invoices 30.4.X5 ...... Initials ......
Name ...... Comments ...... Date ......

CURRENT	30 DAY	60 DAY	90 DAY	120+ DAY
£76.62	0	0	0	0

AMOUNT DUE: **76.62**

(ii)

TREE TOP TIMBER LTD
YEW STREET
ASHFORD

STATEMENT

A/C NO: T713

DATE: 28/04/X5

PAGE: 1

TO: Barkers Ltd
Dalmation Road
Wagford

DATE	DETAILS		INVOICES £	CREDITS £
17.1.X5	Invoice	17512	210 51	
16.3.X5	Invoice	17713	15 50	
3.4.X5	Invoice	17820	40 50	
11.4.X5	Invoice	17857	155 60	
21.4.X5	Invoice	17892	350 44	
22.4.X5	Invoice	17911	14 52	
25.4.X5	Invoice	17925	180 14	
26.4.X5	Credit note	CN7751		121 60
27.4.X5	Invoice	18011	215 10	
			1182 31	121 60

Invoice payment approved by ...... Do not pay January & March invoices 30.4.X5 ...... Initials ......
Name ...... Comments ...... Date ......

CURRENT	30 day	60 day	90 day	120 +
834.70	15.50	0	210.51	0

AMOUNT DUE: **1060.71**

30 days net
5% discount within 7 days of invoice date
2% discount within 14 days of invoice date

(b) This claim covers Win A Lot's expenses during April.

```
                         BARKERS LTD

EXPENSES CLAIM - PROFESSIONAL STAFF
NAME   Win. A. Lot                   MONTH    April

                              NET         VAT        TOTAL
                              £           £          £
MOTOR CAR EXPENSES
   Parking                   14.00                   14.00
   Repairs/Service
   Car Tax
   Insurance
   Petrol                    56.50       9.89        66.39
                             70.50       9.89        80.39

OTHER TRAVEL COSTS
   Taxi                      12.00        —          12.00

OTHER -entertaining, subsistence, etc
   Dinner - The Dog Bowl -
   Subsistence               55.00       9.63        64.63

TOTAL CLAIMED               137.50      19.52       157.02

Claimant's signature    Win A Lot
Authorised by _____
```

(c) The following invoice was received at the end of April.

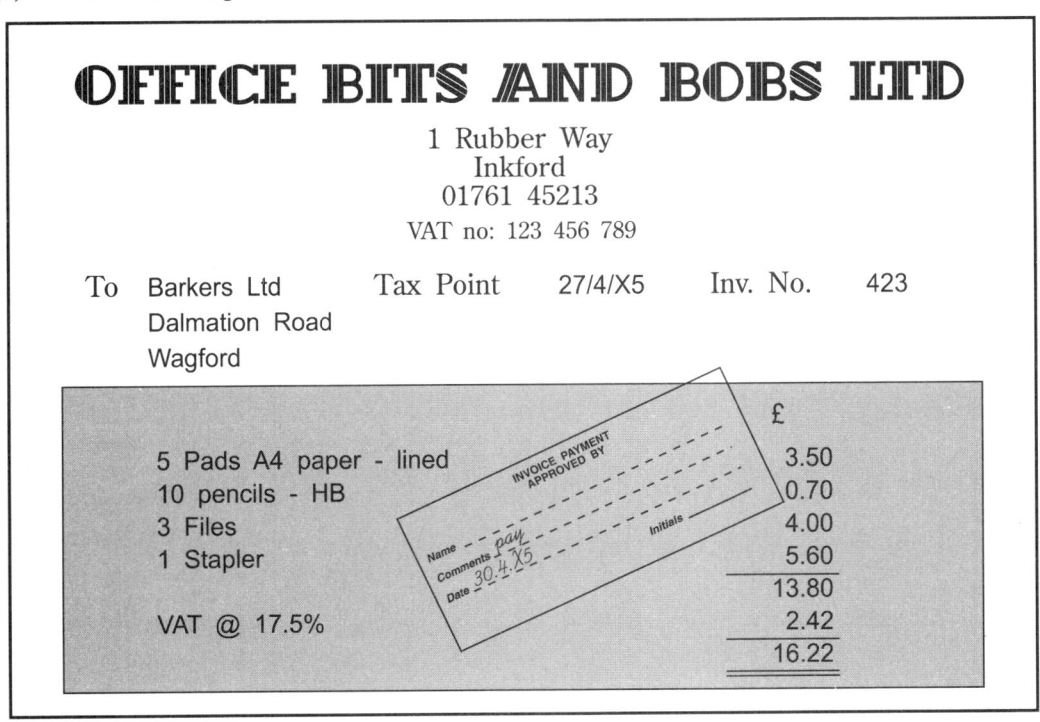

OFFICE BITS AND BOBS LTD

1 Rubber Way
Inkford
01761 45213
VAT no: 123 456 789

To   Barkers Ltd   Tax Point   27/4/X5   Inv. No.   423
     Dalmation Road
     Wagford

	£
5 Pads A4 paper - lined	3.50
10 pencils - HB	0.70
3 Files	4.00
1 Stapler	5.60
	13.80
VAT @ 17.5%	2.42
	16.22

INVOICE PAYMENT APPROVED BY
Name pay
Comments
Date 30.4.X5
Initials

Trial run devolved assessments

(d) This bank statement covers April 20X5.

Crufts Bank   CONFIDENTIAL

20 Spillers Lane
Wagford

Account: Barkers Ltd
Dalmation Road
Wagford

SHEET NO 79

Telephone 01729 35272

20X5   Statement date 1 May 20X5   Account no 30595713

Date	Details	Withdrawals	Deposits	Balance (£)
1 April	Balance from Sheet no. 78			5140.77
3 April	101095	13.99		
	101097	72.50		5054.28
4 April	CC		1351.21	6405.49
5 April	101093	45.21		6360.28
10 April	101099	179.60		
	101094	352.17		
	101098	55.00		5773.51
18 April	DD British Telecom	120.00		5653.51
21 April	Interest - Deposit account		79.87	5733.38
30 April	SO Doberman Mgt Co (rent)	100.00		
	DD Rates	50.00		
	BACS Salaries	1251.00		
30 April	101100	84.23		4248.15
	Balance to Sheet no. 80			4248.15

Key: **SO** Standing Order **DV** Dividend **CC** Cash &/or Cheques **CGS** Charges **PY** Payroll **INT** Interest
EC Eurocheque **TR** Transfer **CP** Card Purchases **DD** Direct Debit **OD** Overdrawn **ADJ** Adjustment

Note. Cheque no 101100 for £84.23 was to top up the petty cash float.

1: Barkers (data and tasks)

(e) **Receipts for petty cash claims**

```
                    3/4/X5

         Cleaner
         Pay £5.00

         B Growler
```

```
                   10/4/X5

         Cleaner
         Pay £5.00

                  P. Pant
```

```
                   17/4/X5

         Cleaner
         Pay £5.00

                  P. Pant
```

```
                   24/4/X5

         Cleaner
         Pay £5.00

              B Growler
```

```
         Rover's
       Supermarket

       15 04 X5

       Coffee x3    4.52
       Tea x2       5.25
       Sugar x2     2.28

       Total       12.05

          P Pant
```

```
         Rusty's
         Hardware

                         2204X5
       Polish              5.25
       Dusters             3.42
       Window Cleaner      2.50
       Rubbish bags        8.95
       Vacuum bags        10.50

       TOTAL              30.62

          P Pant

       VAT No. 32741562
```

Trial run devolved assessments

Impress Dairy
14782

3-4-X5

10 pints milk
at 39p

£3.90

P Pant

Impress Dairy
14811

10-4-X5

10 pints milk
at 39p

£3.90

P Pant

Impress Dairy
14859

17-4-X5

10 pints milk
at 39p

£3.90

P Pant

Impress Dairy
14883

24-4-X5

10 pints milk
at 39p

£3.90

P Pant

Pedigree Wine Bar
VAT No 41731629

24 April 20X5

Meal for 2   62.78

Win A Lot
(subsistence & entertaining)

Post Office Counters Ltd

22.4.X5

Stamps   2.05
Stamps   3.91

Total   5.96
Amount tendered   6.00
Change   0.04

B Growler

VAT registration 512443291

TRIAL RUN DEVOLVED ASSESSMENT 1
BARKERS

Making and Recording Payments

ANSWER BOOKLET

Documents for use in this Assessment

The documents you will need to prepare the solution are given on the following pages and consist of:

(a) blank remittance advices.
(b) blank payment authorisation stamps.
(c) a blank cheque requisition form.
(d) a blank payment authorisation stamp.
(e) a blank giro credit payment slip.
(f) blank cheques.
(g) a blank payments page from the cash book.
(h) petty cash vouchers.
(i) petty cash book page.
(j) selected main ledger accounts.

Trial run devolved assessments

(a) Remittance advices

(i)

14723				
REMITTANCE ADVICE TO:		Barkers Limited Dalmation Road Wagford 01729 35160		
Account No	Date		Page	
DATE	DETAILS	INVOICES £	CREDIT NOTES £	PAYMENT AMOUNT £

(ii)

14724				
REMITTANCE ADVICE TO:		Barkers Limited Dalmation Road Wagford 01729 35160		
Account No	Date		Page	
DATE	DETAILS	INVOICES	CREDIT NOTES	PAYMENT AMOUNT

(iii)

14725				
REMITTANCE ADVICE TO:		Barkers Limited Dalmation Road Wagford 01729 35160		
Account No	Date		Page	
DATE	DETAILS	INVOICES	CREDIT NOTES	PAYMENT AMOUNT

1: Barkers (answer booklet)

(b) Payment authorisation stamps

    (i) FIFI'S FLUFFY FILLINGS

```
┌─────────────────────────────────────┐
│        INVOICE PAYMENT              │
│          APPROVED BY                │
│  Name    .......................... │
│  Comments  Pay all invoices         │
│  Date      30.4.X5                  │
│                      Initials _____ │
└─────────────────────────────────────┘
```

    (ii) TREE TOP TIMBER LIMITED

```
┌─────────────────────────────────────────────┐
│           INVOICE PAYMENT                   │
│             APPROVED BY                     │
│  Name     ................................  │
│  Comments  Do not pay January and March Invoices │
│  Date      30.4.X5                          │
│                          Initials _____     │
└─────────────────────────────────────────────┘
```

    (iii) NICK'S NAILS

```
┌─────────────────────────────────────┐
│        INVOICE PAYMENT              │
│          APPROVED BY                │
│  Name    .......................... │
│  Comments  Pay all invoices         │
│  Date      30.4.X5                  │
│                      Initials _____ │
└─────────────────────────────────────┘
```

(c) Cheque requisition form

```
┌──────────────────────────────────────────────────┐
│                                         247324   │
│            Cheque Requisition                    │
│                                                  │
│   Date       ..................................  │
│   Payable to ..................................  │
│   Amount     ..................................  │
│   Details    ..................................  │
│              ..................................  │
│              ..................................  │
│   Signed     ..................................  │
└──────────────────────────────────────────────────┘
```

(d) Payment authorisation stamp

```
┌─────────────────────────────────────┐
│        INVOICE PAYMENT              │
│          APPROVED BY                │
│  Name    .......................... │
│  Comments  ..... Pay ............   │
│  Date    30.4.X5 .................  │
│                      Initials _____ │
└─────────────────────────────────────┘
```

Trial run devolved assessments

(e) Bank giro credit payment slip

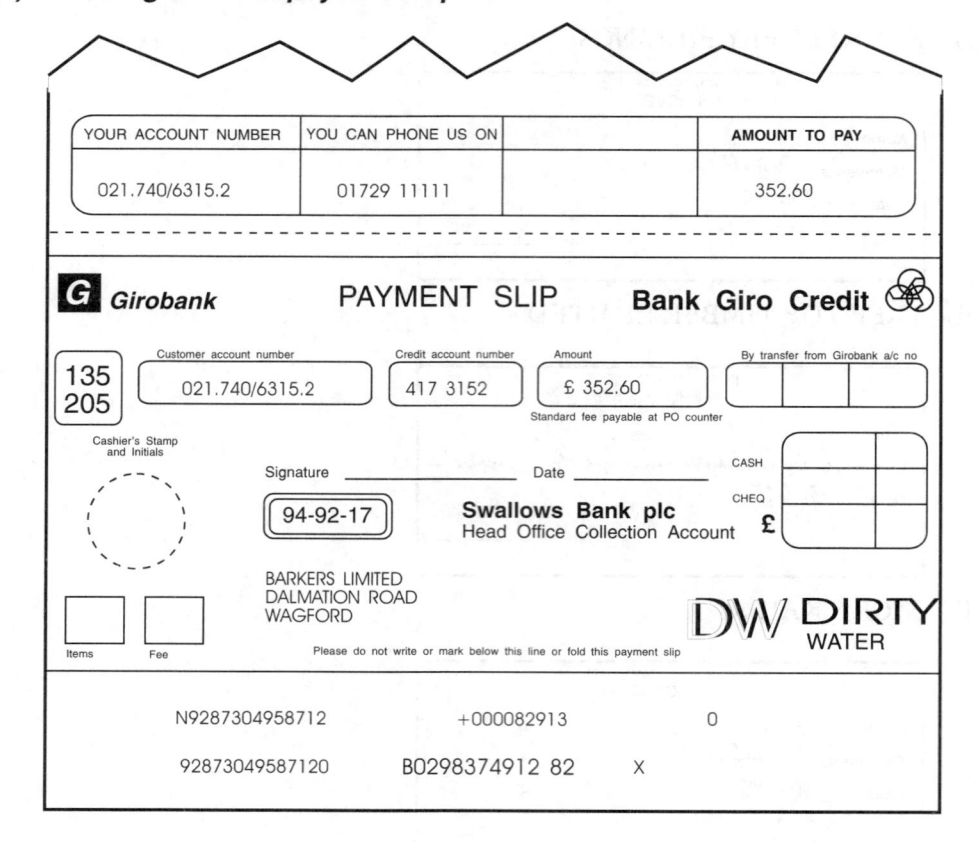

YOUR ACCOUNT NUMBER	YOU CAN PHONE US ON		AMOUNT TO PAY
021.740/6315.2	01729 11111		352.60

G Girobank   PAYMENT SLIP   **Bank Giro Credit**

135
205

Customer account number: 021.740/6315.2
Credit account number: 417 3152
Amount: £ 352.60
Standard fee payable at PO counter
By transfer from Girobank a/c no

Cashier's Stamp and Initials

Signature _____ Date _____

94-92-17

Swallows Bank plc
Head Office Collection Account

CASH
CHEQ
£

BARKERS LIMITED
DALMATION ROAD
WAGFORD

DW DIRTY WATER

Items   Fee

Please do not write or mark below this line or fold this payment slip

N9287304958712   +000082913   0
92873049587120   B0298374912 82   X

(f) Cheques

(i)

Crufts Bank
20 SPILLERS LANE, WAGFORD

_____ 20 ____
20-27-48
CRUFTS BANK PLC

Pay _____ or order

_____

£

FOR AND ON BEHALF OF
BARKERS LIMITED

Cheque No.   Branch No.   Account No.

⑈101101⑈ 20⑈2748⑈ 30595713⑈

(ii)

Crufts Bank
20 SPILLERS LANE, WAGFORD

_____ 20 ____
20-27-48
CRUFTS BANK PLC

Pay _____ or order

_____

£

FOR AND ON BEHALF OF
BARKERS LIMITED

Cheque No.   Branch No.   Account No.

⑈101102⑈ 20⑈2748⑈ 30595713⑈

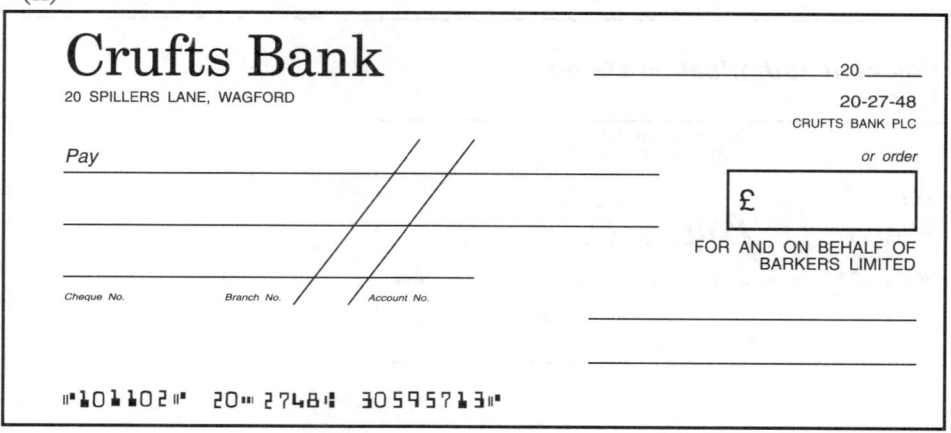

1: Barkers (answer booklet)

(iii)

Crufts Bank
20 SPILLERS LANE, WAGFORD

_____ 20 _____
20-27-48
CRUFTS BANK PLC

Pay _____ or order

£ [   ]

FOR AND ON BEHALF OF
BARKERS LIMITED

Cheque No.   Branch No.   Account No.

⑈101103⑈ 20⎯2748⑈ 30595713⑈

(iv)

Crufts Bank
20 SPILLERS LANE, WAGFORD

_____ 20 _____
20-27-48
CRUFTS BANK PLC

Pay _____ or order

£ [   ]

FOR AND ON BEHALF OF
BARKERS LIMITED

Cheque No.   Branch No.   Account No.

⑈101104⑈ 20⎯2748⑈ 30595713⑈

(v)

Crufts Bank
20 SPILLERS LANE, WAGFORD

_____ 20 _____
20-27-48
CRUFTS BANK PLC

Pay _____ or order

£ [   ]

FOR AND ON BEHALF OF
BARKERS LIMITED

Cheque No.   Branch No.   Account No.

⑈101105⑈ 20⎯2748⑈ 30595713⑈

(vi)

Crufts Bank
20 SPILLERS LANE, WAGFORD

_____ 20 _____
20-27-48
CRUFTS BANK PLC

Pay _____ or order

£ [   ]

FOR AND ON BEHALF OF
BARKERS LIMITED

Cheque No.   Branch No.   Account No.

⑈101106⑈ 20⎯2748⑈ 30595713⑈

Trial run devolved assessments

(g) Manual cash book: payments

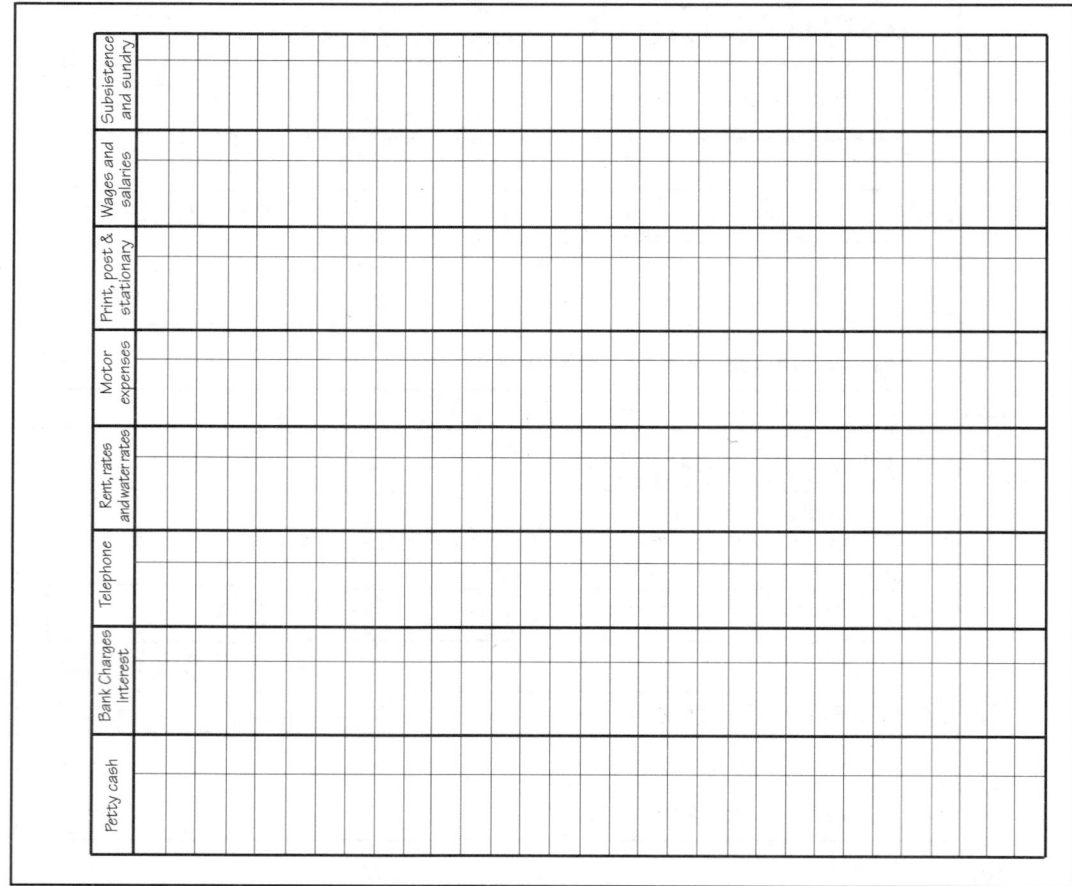

Date	Details	Cheque number	Discounts Received	Total	VAT	Creditors	Petty cash	Bank Charges Interest	Telephone	Rent, rates and water rates	Motor expenses	Print, post & stationary	Wages and salaries	Subsistence and sundry
1														
2														
3														
4														
5														
6														
7														
8														
9														
10														
11														
12														
13														
14														
15														
16														
17														
18														
19														
20														
21														
22														
23														
24														
25														
26														
27														
28														
29														
30														

APRIL - PAYMENTS

(h) Petty cash vouchers

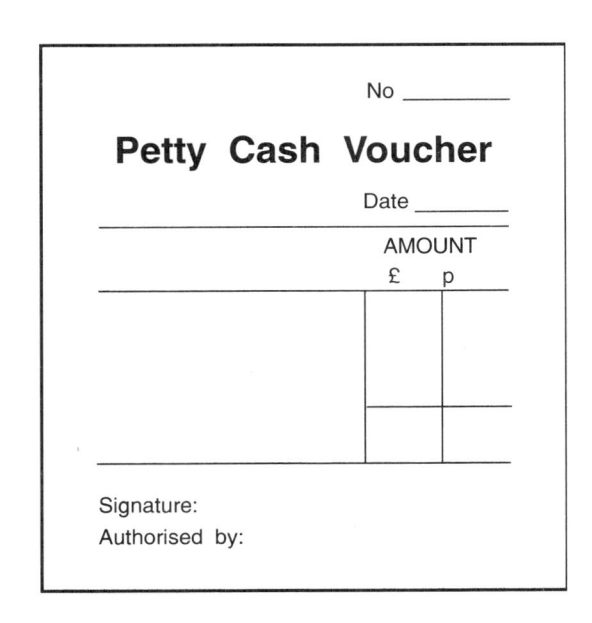

No ________

Petty Cash Voucher

Date ________

	AMOUNT £	p

Signature:
Authorised by:

No ________

Petty Cash Voucher

Date ________

	AMOUNT £	p

Signature:
Authorised by:

No ________

Petty Cash Voucher

Date ________

	AMOUNT £	p

Signature:
Authorised by:

No ________

Petty Cash Voucher

Date ________

	AMOUNT £	p

Signature:
Authorised by:

No ________

Petty Cash Voucher

Date ________

	AMOUNT £	p

Signature:
Authorised by:

No ________

Petty Cash Voucher

Date ________

	AMOUNT £	p

Signature:
Authorised by:

Trial run devolved assessments

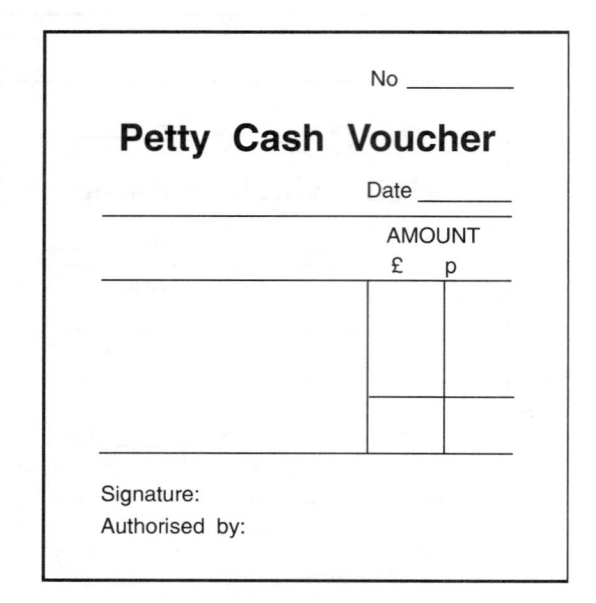

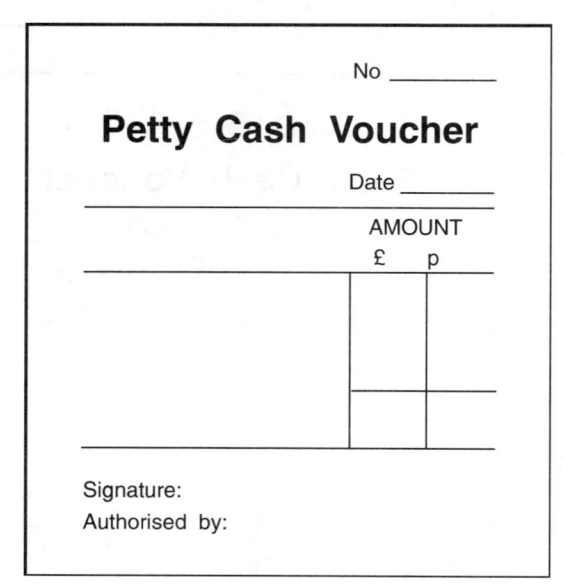

Petty Cash Voucher No _____ Date _____ AMOUNT £ p Signature: Authorised by:	**Petty Cash Voucher** No _____ Date _____ AMOUNT £ p Signature: Authorised by:
Petty Cash Voucher No _____ Date _____ AMOUNT £ p Signature: Authorised by:	**Petty Cash Voucher** No _____ Date _____ AMOUNT £ p Signature: Authorised by:
Petty Cash Voucher No _____ Date _____ AMOUNT £ p Signature: Authorised by:	**Petty Cash Voucher** No _____ Date _____ AMOUNT £ p Signature: Authorised by:

1: Barkers (answer booklet)

(i) Petty cash book page

			PETTY CASH BOOK						Analysis of payments			
Details	Net receipt £	VAT £	Total £	Date	Details	Voucher No	Total £	VAT £	Wages & salaries £	Subsistence and sundry £	Print, post and stationery £
Balance b/f			100.00								

Trial run devolved assessments

(j)   Main ledger accounts

Creditors account

Date	Details	Amount	Date	Details	Amount
		£			£
30 April 20X5	Purchase returns day book	133.10	1 April 20X5	Balance b/f	226.01
			30 April 20X5	Purchase day book	1,380.52

Print, post and stationery

Date	Details	Amount	Date	Details	Amount
		£			£
1 April 20X5	Balance b/f	40.56			

Rent, rates and water rates

Date	Details	Amount	Date	Details	Amount
		£			£
1 April 20X5	Balance b/f	654.37			

1: Barkers (answer booklet)

Telephone

Date	Details	Amount £	Date	Details	Amount £
1 April 20X5	Balance b/f	452 84			

Motor expenses

Date	Details	Amount £	Date	Details	Amount £
1 April 20X5	Balance b/f	212 80			

Wages and salaries

Date	Details	Amount £	Date	Details	Amount £
1 April 20X5	Balance b/f	6,850 25			

Subsistence and sundry

Date	Details	Amount £	Date	Details	Amount £
1 April 20X5	Balance b/f	473.48			

VAT

Date	Details	Amount £	Date	Details	Amount £
30 April 20X5	Purchase day book	181.43	1 April 20X5	Balance b/f	586.48
			30 April 20X5	Sales day book	352.51
			30 April 20X5	Cash book receipts	200.51

Discounts received

Date	Details	Amount £	Date	Details	Amount £
			1 April 20X5	Balance b/f	121.07

1: Barkers (answer booklet)

Workings

TRIAL RUN DEVOLVED ASSESSMENT 2
BEST-BOOKS

FOUNDATION STAGE - NVQ/SVQ2

Unit 2

Making and Recording Payments

The purpose of this Trial Run Devolved Assessment is to give you an idea of what an AAT simulation looks like. It is not intended as a definitive guide to the tasks you may be required to perform.

The suggested time allowance for this Assessment is **two hours**. Up to 30 minutes extra time may be permitted in an AAT simulation. Breaks in assessment will be allowed in the AAT simulation, but it must normally be completed in one day.

Calculators may be used but no reference material is permitted.

DO NOT OPEN THIS PAPER UNTIL YOU ARE READY TO START UNDER TIMED CONDITIONS

Trial run devolved assessments

INSTRUCTIONS

This Assessment is designed to test your ability to record and account for cash transactions.

The situation is provided on Page 117.

You are provided with data on Pages 119 to 124 which you must use to complete the related tasks on Page 118.

Your answers should be set out in this booklet using the documents provided. You may require additional answer pages.

You are allowed two hours to complete your work.

A high level of accuracy is required. Check your work carefully.

Correcting fluid may be used but should be used in moderation. Errors should be crossed out neatly and clearly. You should write in black ink, not pencil.

You are advised to read the whole of the Assessment before commencing as all of the information may be of value and is not necessarily supplied in the sequence in which you might wish to deal with it.

A full suggested solution to this Assessment is provided on Page 231 of this Kit.

THE SITUATION

Your name is Alan Murray and you are employed as an accounts clerk, in a regional book shop, for a chain of book shops throughout the country. You are employed in the North West Regional office at 101, Blackburn Road, Preston PR1 2HE and today's date is Monday 12 May 20X7. The name of the organisation is Best-Books Ltd.

The business

The North West Regional Office co-ordinates the commercial activities of 10 book shops throughout the North of England involving a range of customers from academic institutions, college and university lecturers and individuals.

Books are zero-rated for VAT purposes.

Expenditure

Suppliers' invoices come initially to you for checking before passing to your supervisor John Ross for authorisation.

Once suppliers' invoices have been checked and authorised they are passed to you to prepare the cheques which will then be signed by the Company Accountant, Michael Christian.

You also have to balance off the creditors and debtors ledgers, each month and provide a reconciliation between individual creditors ledgers and suppliers statements of account.

Petty cash

Each month you are presented with approved payments from petty cash which you have to enter in the petty cash book. The imprest account has a float of £150.

Cash and bank

One of the tasks you undertake is to balance off the cash book for each of the shops within the region on a monthly basis.

Trial run devolved assessments

THE TASKS TO BE PERFORMED

		Blank document on page(s)
1	Check the invoices received for payment, on 12 May, prior to passing to John Ross for authorisation. Explain, where appropriate, any corrective action you would wish to take.	120
2	You are required to prepare the necessary cheques, for subsequent signature by the Company Accountant.	121
3	Balance the ledger accounts of Pronto Press Ltd as at 30/04/X7.	122
4	Reconcile the statement from Pronto Press Ltd with the creditors ledger account as at 30/04/X7.	–
5	Enter the details of petty cash payments made in April 20X7 into the petty cash book and enter the cash drawn from the bank at the end of the month to make up the imprest.	123
6	Prepare the two column cash book for the Blackpool shop for April 20X7, including carrying down the balances, at 30/04/X7.	124

2: Best-Books (data, tasks and answer booklet)

DATA

Suppliers invoices received on 12 May 20X7

Invoice

PRONTO PRESS LTD
107 Wimbledon Place
London EC2 1AR

Best-Books Ltd
101 Blackburn Road
Preston

Invoice No. 1231
Date/Tax point: 14.04.X7

Item Description	Quantity	Unit price £ p	Total £ p
Chemistry A Level	53 copies	11.99	635.47
Physics A Level	101 copies	8.95	903.95
			1539.42

Terms: 5%, 30 days

Invoice

SUPER STATIONERY SUPPLIES LTD
94 Chester Road
Chester

Best-Books Ltd
101 Blackburn Road
Preston

Invoice No. 604
Date/Tax point: 08.05.X7

Item Description	Quantity	Unit price £ p	Total £ p
Staples	53 boxes	2.58	136.74
Discount (10%)			13.67
Net			123.07
VAT (17½%)			23.93
			147.00

Trial run devolved assessments

	Invoice		
	BEAUTIFUL BOOKS PLC		
	16 Grosvenor Avenue Blackburn		
Best-Books Ltd 101 Blackburn Road Preston		Invoice No. 131 Date/Tax point: 07.05.X7	
Item Description	Quantity	Unit price £ p	Total £ p
Accounting for Beginners Law for the Non-legal Person	35 copies 28 copies	16.95 8.95	586.25 250.60
			836.85
Terms: 3%, 30 days			

Internal report on suppliers' invoices

Suppliers invoices to check	Action

Cheques authorised

The following cheques have been authorised, by J Ross, for preparation prior to signature by the Company Accountant, Michael Christian.

Name	Amount
	£
The National Book Shop	690.40
Open Learning Ltd	248.26
Simpsons Stationers	140.50

Date _____

Payee _____

£ [   ]

LANCS BANK PLC 30-60-58
High Street, Preston

_____ 20 _____

Pay _____ or order

£ [   ]

Best-Books Ltd

Cheque Number   Branch number   Account Number
200101   306058   60711348

Date _____

Payee _____

£ [   ]

LANCS BANK PLC 30-60-58
High Street, Preston

_____ 20 _____

Pay _____ or order

£ [   ]

Best-Books Ltd

Cheque Number   Branch number   Account Number
200102   306058   60711348

Date _____

Payee _____

£ [   ]

LANCS BANK PLC 30-60-58
High Street, Preston

_____ 20 _____

Pay _____ or order

£ [   ]

Best-Books Ltd

Cheque Number   Branch number   Account Number
200103   306058   60711348

Trial run devolved assessments

Pronto Press Ltd

Creditors ledger

PRONTO PRESS LTD

		£			£
14 April	Bank	105.40	1 April	Bal b/d	294.51
19 April	Bank	110.62	8 April	Purchases	206.48
26 April	Bank	1,848.08	14 April	Purchases	1,539.42
			10 April	Purchases	194.69

Statement of account

Statement of Account

PRONTO PRESS LTD

CUSTOMER
Best-Books Ltd

Tel: 01772 604903
Date: 30 April 20X7

Date	Reference	Debit £ p	Credit £ p	Balance £ p
1 April	B/d			294.51
10 April	Purchase	206.48		500.99
16 April	Purchase	1539.42		2040.41
16 April	Bank		105.40	1935.01
21 April	Bank		110.62	1824.39

Details of petty cash payments for month ending 30/04/X7

Date	Details	Amount £
1 April	Telephone	2.40
7 April	Postage	8.29
8 April	Travel	11.40
10 April	Postage	9.30
12 April	Newspapers	1.49
17 April	Tea/coffee	6.45
20 April	Milk	2.19
24 April	Postage	8.90
24 April	Travel	4.25
27 April	Postage	11.98
30 April	Milk	2.19

Petty cash book

Receipts	Date	Details	Amount
£			£
Bal b/d 150.00			
Bal b/d			
Bank _____			
Bal c/d _____			

Transactions for the Blackpool shop for April 20X7

			£
April	1	Balances	
		Cash in hand	21.90
		Bank (overdrawn)	101.45
April	2	Stationery (paid cash)	11.50
	5	Suppliers paid by cheque	891.56
	8	Cash to bank	200.00
	11	Suppliers paid by cheque	196.51
	15	Salaries by cheque	296.50
	16	PAYE and NI by cheque to Inland Revenue	290.61
	19	Cash to bank	300.00
	24	Suppliers paid by cheque	490.65
	28	Cash to bank	100.00
	28	Total receipts	
		Cash	659.26
		Bank	2,217.44

Trial run devolved assessments

Two column cash book

Date	Details	Cash £	Bank £	Date	Details	Cash £	Bank £

TRIAL RUN DEVOLVED ASSESSMENT 3
GROW-EASY

FOUNDATION STAGE - NVQ/SVQ2

Unit 2

Making and Recording Payments

The purpose of this Trial Run Devolved Assessment is to give you an idea of what an AAT simulation looks like. It is not intended as a definitive guide to the tasks you may be required to perform.

The suggested time allowance for this Assessment is **two hours**. Up to 30 minutes extra time may be permitted in an AAT simulation. Breaks in assessment will be allowed in the AAT simulation, but it must normally be completed in one day.

Calculators may be used but no reference material is permitted.

DO NOT OPEN THIS PAPER UNTIL YOU ARE READY TO START UNDER TIMED CONDITIONS

Trial run devolved assessments

INSTRUCTIONS

This Assessment is designed to test your ability to record and account for cash transactions.

The situation is provided on Page 127.

You are provided with data on Pages 129 to 136 which you must use to complete the related tasks on Page 128.

Your answers should be set out on Pages 129 to 136 using the documents provided. You may require additional answer pages.

You are allowed two hours to complete your work.

A high level of accuracy is required. Check your work carefully.

Correcting fluid may be used but should be used in moderation. Errors should be crossed out neatly and clearly. You should write in black ink, not pencil.

You are advised to read the whole of the Assessment before commencing as all of the information may be of value and is not necessarily supplied in the sequence in which you might wish to deal with it.

A full suggested solution to this Assessment is provided on Page 237 of this Kit.

3: Grow-Easy (data, tasks and answer booklet)

THE SITUATION

Your name is Simon Dutton and you are the accounts clerk for a medium sized garden centre, Grow-Easy Ltd, 25 Parkside, Kendal LA9 7BL, in the north of England.

Today is Thursday 24 April 20X7.

The business

The company sells a variety of plants produced from the Grow-Easy Nursery and a range of garden tools, implements and garden ornaments. It has also started to make a small range of wooden garden furniture. Although some sales are credit sales the significant majority of the sales are for cash within the garden centre itself. The firm is below the compulsory registration limit for VAT and consequently has not registered.

Expenditure

One of your duties is making out cheques to pay suppliers. You are not an authorised signatory on the company bank account and once you have made out the cheque they are passed, by you, to the company accountant Shaun Moss for his signature.

One of your other tasks is to reconcile the company's suppliers accounts statements with the purchase ledger accounts and reconcile the company's bank statement with the cash book on a regular basis.

Petty cash

Petty cash is maintained on an imprest system with a weekly float of £100. Staff cannot claim reimbursement from petty cash unless they complete a petty cash voucher and supply a receipt.

You can authorise payments from petty cash yourself provided they do not exceed £10, otherwise you must first seek the Company Accountant's authorisation.

Trial run devolved assessments

THE TASKS TO BE PERFORMED

		Blank document on page(s)
1	You are required to prepare cheques, for subsequent signature, by the company accountant.	129 - 131
2	Reconcile the statements for Anglia Timber Ltd and J Caton and Co with the ledger accounts, as at 31.3.X7.	–
3	The company's bank statement for the month ending 31 March is enclosed alongside details of the company's monthly standing orders. You are required to check the bank statements to ensure that all standing orders are correct and to explain what action you would taken in respect of any discrepancies.	134
4	You are required to check the claims for petty cash expenditure and indicate what action you would take with each.	135
5	Post the entries for 24 April 20X7 to the petty cash book, and balance off the accounts, with the entries necessary to top up the imprest account.	136

3: Grow-Easy (data, tasks and answer booklet)

DATA

Cheques to suppliers

The following cheques to suppliers have been authorised by Shaun Moss on 24 April 20X7.

Name	Amount £
Anglian Timber Ltd	741.26
J Priestley Seedlings Ltd	64.96
J Caton and Co	79.47
South Lakeland District Council	101.70
Fine Furnishings Ltd	74.61
Harry Rumsden Wholesalers	139.55

All of the above cheques have been agreed for preparation by Shaun Moss, the company accountant.

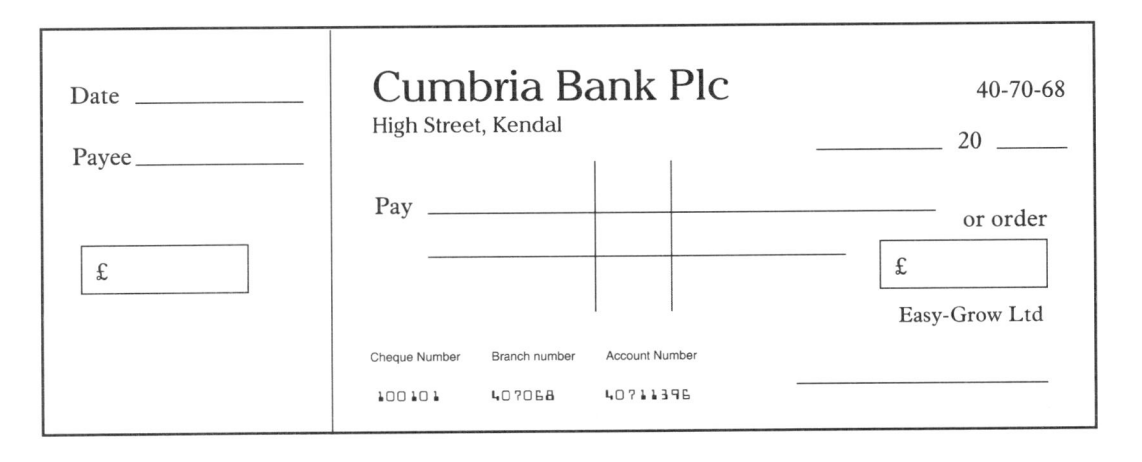

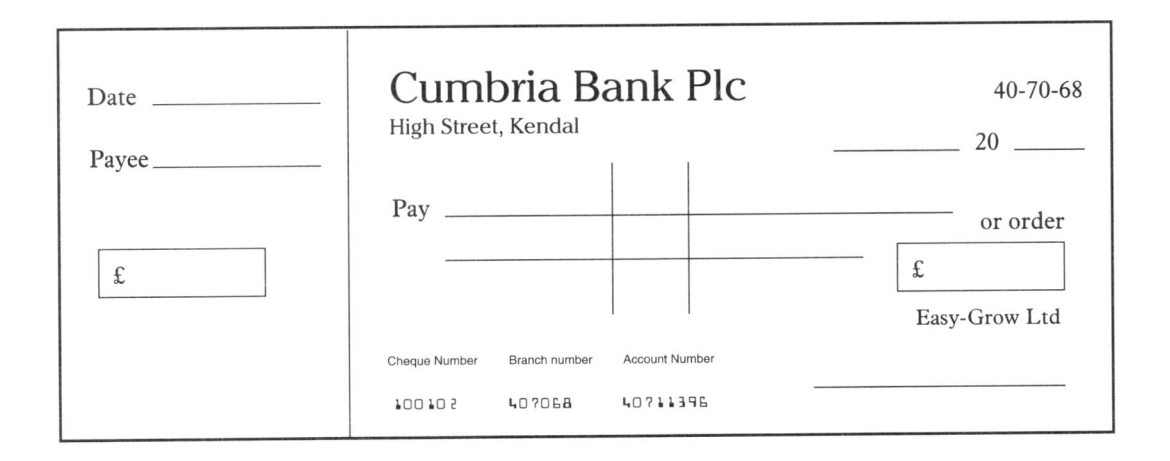

```
Date _____           Cumbria Bank Plc              40-70-68
Payee _____           High Street, Kendal
                                                     _____ 20 _____
                       Pay _____
 £                         _____ or order
                                                         £
                                                    Easy-Grow Ltd
                       Cheque Number  Branch number  Account Number
                         100101         407068         40711396
```

```
Date _____           Cumbria Bank Plc              40-70-68
Payee _____           High Street, Kendal
                                                     _____ 20 _____
                       Pay _____
 £                         _____ or order
                                                         £
                                                    Easy-Grow Ltd
                       Cheque Number  Branch number  Account Number
                         100102         407068         40711396
```

Trial run devolved assessments

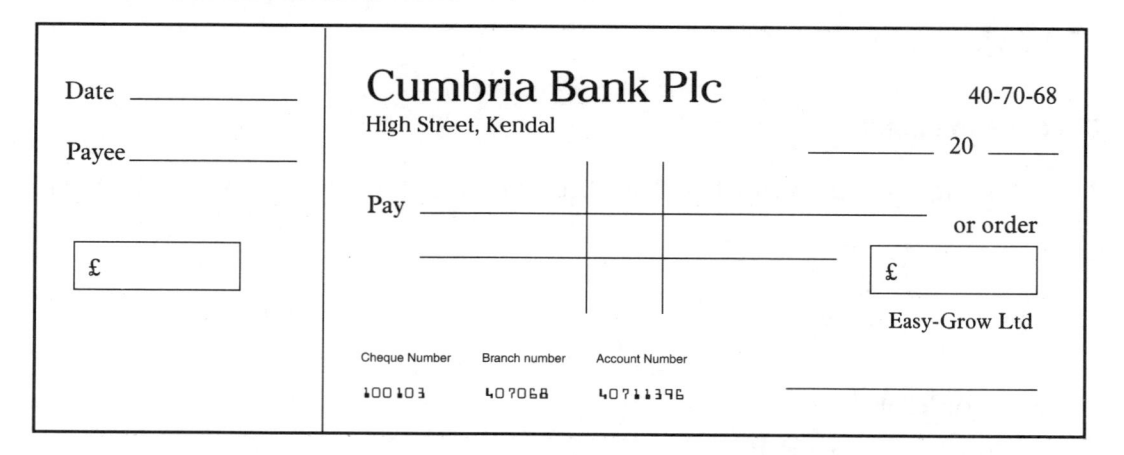

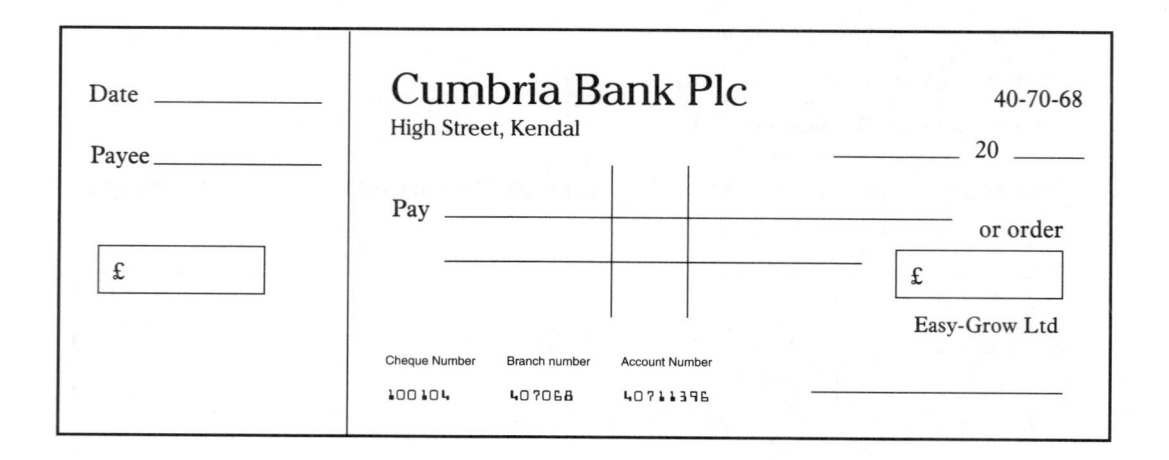

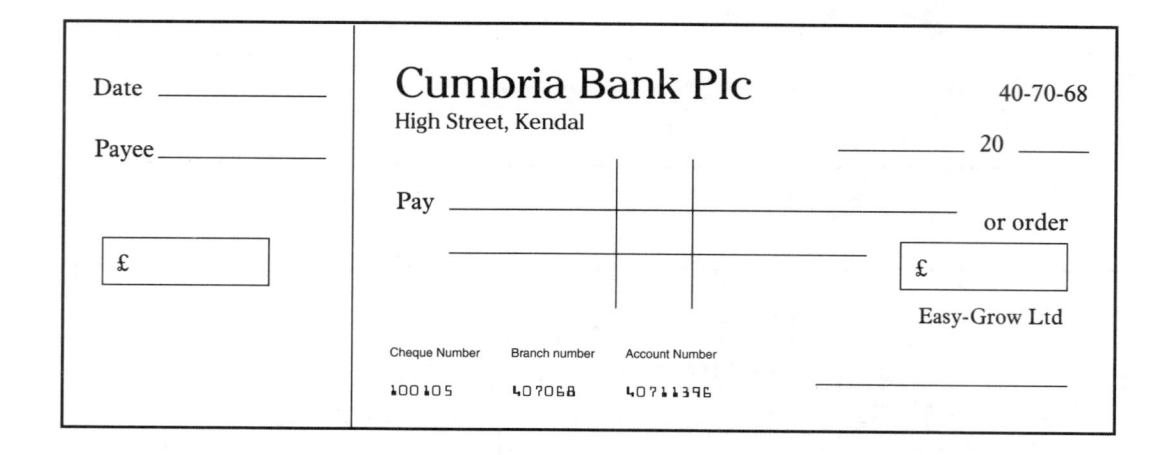

Cumbria Bank Plc
High Street, Kendal

Date _____
Payee _____
£ _____

Pay _____ or order
_____
£ _____
Easy-Grow Ltd

20 _____
40-70-68

Cheque Number: 100103
Branch number: 407068
Account Number: 40711396

Cumbria Bank Plc
High Street, Kendal

Date _____
Payee _____
£ _____

Pay _____ or order
_____
£ _____
Easy-Grow Ltd

20 _____
40-70-68

Cheque Number: 100104
Branch number: 407068
Account Number: 40711396

Cumbria Bank Plc
High Street, Kendal

Date _____
Payee _____
£ _____

Pay _____ or order
_____
£ _____
Easy-Grow Ltd

20 _____
40-70-68

Cheque Number: 100105
Branch number: 407068
Account Number: 40711396

| Date _____ | **Cumbria Bank Plc** | 40-70-68 |
| Payee _____ | High Street, Kendal | _____ 20 _____ |

Pay _____ or order

£ [   ]   £ [   ]

Easy-Grow Ltd

Cheque Number   Branch number   Account Number
100106   407068   40711396

Anglian Timber Ltd

Statement of account

ANGLIAN TIMBER LTD
Tel: 01539 725786

STATEMENT OF ACCOUNT

DATE: 31 March 20X7

CUSTOMER
Grow-Easy Ltd

DATE	REFERENCE	DEBIT	CREDIT	BALANCE
1 March 20X7				609.43
15 March 20X7	Inv 006942	1,143.17		
17 March 20X7	Inv 006951	1,107.93		2,860.53
27 March 20X7	Bank		1,741.26	1,119.27

Purchase ledger account

ANGLIAN TIMBER LTD

		March 20X7 £			*March 20X7* £
12 March	Returns	79.10	Balance b/d		609.43
24 March	Bank	1,741.26	17 March	Purchases	1,143.17
	Balance c/d	1,040.17	19 March	Purchases	1,107.93
		2,860.53			2,860.53
			Balance b/d		1,040.17

Trial run devolved assessments

Caton and Co

Statement of account

J CATON AND CO
Tel: 017683 40972

STATEMENT OF ACCOUNT
DATE: 31 March 20X7

CUSTOMER
Grow-Easy Ltd

DATE	REFERENCE	DEBIT	CREDIT	BALANCE
1 March 20X7				179.47
27 March 20X7	Bank		179.47	
29 March 20X7	Inv 609401	108.50		108.50

Purchase ledger account

J CATON AND CO

	March 20X7 £		March 20X7 £
24 March Bank	179.47	Balance b/d	179.47
Balance c/d	-		-
	179.47		179.47
		Balance b/d	-

Bank statement

```
┌─────────────────────────────────────────────────────────────────────────┐
│  Cumbria Bank Plc                              CONFIDENTIAL             │
├─────────────────────────────────────────────────────────────────────────┤
│  High Street                Account  Grow-Easy      SHEET NO  131       │
│  Kendal                                                                 │
│  Telephone  01542 111 2222                                              │
│                                                                         │
│  20X7                       Statement date  19 March    Account no 40711396 │
└─────────────────────────────────────────────────────────────────────────┘
```

Date	Details	Payments (£)	Receipts (£)	Balance (£)
1 March				256.06 OD
7 March		243.45		499.51 OD
9 March			1006.59	507.08
12 March	SO Electricity	79.00		428.08
18 March		1143.17		715.09 OD
18 March	SO Gas Board	95.00		810.09 OD
19 March			2391.74	1581.65
19 March		1107.93		473.72
20 March			1983.46	2457.18
22 March	SO BT	200.00		2257.18
25 March		179.47		2077.71
28 March			1741.26	3818.97

Key					
SO Standing Order	**DV** Dividend	**CC** Cash &/or Cheques	**CGS** Charges	**PY** Payroll	**INT** Interest
EC Eurocheque	**TR** Transfer	**CP** Card Purchases	**DD** Direct Debit	**OD** Overdrawn	**ADJ** Adjustment

Details of company standing orders

1. *Northern Electricity Board.* Direct debit payable on 12th of each month for £79.00.

2. *Northern Gas Board.* The annual payment of £1,260.00 is payable in 12 equal instalments on the 18th of each month.

3. *British Telecom* standing order of £2,400.00 for a full year divided into 12 equal instalments on the 22nd of each month.

Trial run devolved assessments

Standing orders	Action

Petty cash vouchers

Petty Cash Voucher

Date 24/04/X7

	AMOUNT £	p
Postage	7	40
	7	40

Signature: *J Barnes*
Authorised by:

Petty Cash Voucher

Date 24/04/X7

	AMOUNT £	p
Postage	4	90
	4	90

Signature: *J Barnes*
Authorised by:

Petty Cash Voucher

Date 24/04/X7

	AMOUNT £	p
Stationery	14	95
	14	95

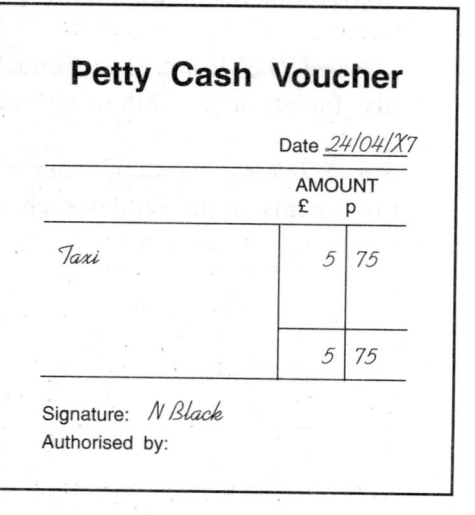

Signature: *C Loftus*
Authorised by:

Petty Cash Voucher

Date 24/04/X7

	AMOUNT £	p
Taxi	5	75
	5	75

Signature: *N Black*
Authorised by:

POST OFFICE COUNTERS

Received with thanks

Stamps   £7.40

Date   24/04/X7

JIM'S TAXIS

Received with thanks

Office to station   £5.75

Date   24/04/X7

ALPHA STATIONERY STORE

Received with thanks

Files   £14.95

Date   24/04/X7

Petty cash voucher	Action

Trial run devolved assessments

Petty cash book

Date 20X7	Postage £	Travel/taxis £	Stationery £	General £	Total £
17 April B/d: Receipt					(100.00)
18 April	2.40	6.90	-	2.00	11.30
19 April	4.90	14.10	6.75	11.45	37.20
20 April	1.20	-	2.25	1.05	4.50
21 April	-	-	2.90	-	2.90
22 April	1.10	1.25	0.90	-	3.25
23 April	2.40	1.15	2.00	1.00	6.55
Totals	═══	═══	═══	═══	═══
24 April Balance c/d					
25 April Balance b/d Bank					100.00

TRIAL RUN DEVOLVED ASSESSMENT 4
WORKBASE OFFICE SUPPLIES

FOUNDATION STAGE - NVQ/SVQ2

Unit 2

Making and Recording Payments

The purpose of this Trial Run Devolved Assessment is to give you an idea of what an AAT simulation looks like. It is not intended as a definitive guide to the tasks you may be required to perform.

The suggested time allowance for this Assessment is **two hours**. Up to 30 minutes extra time may be permitted in an AAT simulation. Breaks in assessment will be allowed in the AAT simulation, but it must normally be completed in one day.

Calculators may be used but no reference material is permitted.

DO NOT OPEN THIS PAPER UNTIL YOU ARE READY TO START UNDER TIMED CONDITIONS

Trial run devolved assessments

INSTRUCTIONS

This Assessment is designed to test your ability to record and account for credit transactions.

The situation is provided on Page 139.

You are provided with data on Pages 140 – 147 which you must use to complete the related tasks on Pages 140 - 147.

Your answers should be set out on Pages 140 - 147 using the documents provided. You may require additional answer pages.

You are allowed two hours to complete your work.

A high level of accuracy is required. Check your work carefully.

Correcting fluid may be used but should be used in moderation. Errors should be crossed out neatly and clearly. You should write in black ink, not pencil.

You are advised to read the whole of the Assessment before commencing as all of the information may be of value and is not necessarily supplied in the sequence in which you might wish to deal with it.

A full suggested solution to this Assessment is provided on Page 243 of this Kit.

THE SITUATION

Your employer is Workbase Office Supplies Ltd ('Workbase'), a supplier of office equipment, mainly to business customers, with a single sales office based in Liverpool.

All deliveries are entered in a deliveries book in which each separate delivery is allocated a GRN number. Most of Workbase's suppliers provide delivery notes which are signed by Workbase's goods inwards staff. Some of the suppliers offer settlement discounts.

Suppliers' invoices are numbered on receipt. Purchases and purchase returns are recorded in a single day book. There is no separate purchase returns book.

All the company's supplies attract VAT at 17.5%. VAT is rounded down to the nearest penny.

Personnel include:

Mr Denton	General Manager
Ms Lang	Warehouse Manager
Mrs Tarvey	Chief Buyer

You work in a department running both sales and purchase ledgers.

When suppliers' invoices are received you are required to validate them. This includes checking them against goods received documentation (which should be signed by the warehouse manager) and purchase orders (which should be signed by the chief buyer), and checking their numerical accuracy (including discounts and VAT).

You are responsible for the maintenance of the purchase day book, and the purchase ledger. Note that any adjustments to the ledger accounts, other than those which derive from routine postings from the books of prime record, must be authorised in writing by the General Manager.

Trial run devolved assessments

THE TASKS TO BE PERFORMED

TASK 1

Under current procedures, the various checks carried out on suppliers' invoices are evidenced by means of a tick on the invoice. Any queries, inaccurate invoices and invoices for which there is no GRN are passed to Mr Denton for further action.

Mr Denton is concerned that suppliers' invoices may not always be checked thoroughly, and wants the procedure to be improved.

Design a 'rubber stamp' which can be entered on incoming invoices to show that each of the checks necessary has been carried out. Try to think of as many different checks as possible. Include 'tick boxes' on the stamp for each check (where appropriate). Among the procedures to be carried out is the checking of purchase orders. The stamp should also have a space for initialling by the person authorising payment.

TASK 2

On Pages 140 to 145 are suppliers' invoices passed to you for processing, together with related purchase orders and goods received notes.

You are required to perform your usual validation checks on the invoices. Any invoices which do not pass the validation checks should be notified to the general manager by means of a memo setting out details of the invoices, the reasons for not passing them and your intended action in each case. Use the memo form on Page 146.

KINETON LTD
4 Hythe March
Readwich RL2
0123 714822

Invoice: 403728
Date: 28/8/X5
Your ref: 7324

To: Workbase Office Supplies Ltd
63 Conduit St
Liverpool LI 6NN

VAT Reg. 4111 3286

Description	Quantity	Price £	Total £	Discount £	Net amount £
Cardboard packaging	100 kg	0.78	78.00	5% 3.90	74.10

Terms
Net, 30 days

Total goods	74.10
VAT @ 17.5%	12.96
Amount due	87.06

BEACON LTD
The Industrial Complex
Beaver Court
Wigan

To: Workbase Office Supplies Ltd
63 Conduit St
Liverpool Ll 6NN

Invoice: 117382
Date: 27/8/X5

Tel: 01142 314281
Fax: 01142 314280

VAT Reg. 1112 3468

Description	Quantity	Price £	Total £	Discount £	Net amount £
Grey filing cabinets	4	150.00	600.00	15% 90.00	510.00
Cream filing cabinets	2	150.00	300.00	45.00	255.00

Terms
Net, 30 days

Total goods	765.00
VAT @ 17.5%	133.87
Amount due	898.87

WESTON SUPPLIES
43-47 Park Drive Rd
Leeds LS7 1PA
Tel: 0113 292 4738

To: Workbase Office Supplies Ltd
63 Conduit St
Liverpool Ll 6NN

I10743
Date: 27/8/X5

VAT Reg. 2 173 7728

Description	Quantity	Price £	Total £	Discount £	Net amount £
Ballpoints - black (50)	100	3.00	300.00	10% 30.00	270.00
Ballpoints - blue (50)	100	3.00	300.00	30.00	270.00

Terms
Net, 30 days

Total goods	540.00
VAT @ 17.5%	94.50
Amount due	634.50

RYEMEAD LTD
140 Lisbon Way
Reading, Berks

Invoice: 9942
Date: 26/8/X5

Tel: 01423 710020

To: Workbase Office Supplies Ltd
    63 Conduit St
    Liverpool Ll 6NN

VAT Reg. 4 427 0013

Description	Quantity	Price £	Total £	Discount £	Net amount £
Filing Trays: Smoke	20	8.50	170.00	20% 34.00	136.00
Filing Trays: Grey	10	8.50	85.00	17.00	68.00
Filing Trays: Slate blue	5	8.50	85.00	17.00	68.00

Terms
Net, 30 days

Total goods	272.00
VAT @ 17.5%	47.60
Amount due	319.60

HARBORD LTD
Grange Industrial Estate
Units 7-9
Grange Lane
Portsmouth PL2 1PR

Inv: 11324876
Date: 26/8/X5

Tel: 0172 117 320

To: Workbase Office Supplies Ltd
    63 Conduit St
    Liverpool Ll 6NN

VAT Reg. 6 176 2660

Description	Quantity	Price £	Total £	Discount £	Net amount £
Typist's chair - Paprika	5	95.00	475.00	15% 71.25	403.75

Terms
Net, 30 days

Total goods	403.75
VAT @ 17.5%	70.65
Amount due	474.40

WORKBASE OFFICE SUPPLIES LTD
63 Conduit Street
Liverpool L1 6NN

PURCHASE ORDER
P07324

19/8/X5

Supplier
Kineton Ltd

Cardboard Packaging - 100kg @ 78 pence per kg.
Discount 5%

J Tarvey

WORKBASE OFFICE SUPPLIES LTD
63 Conduit Street
Liverpool L1 6NN

PURCHASE ORDER
P07331

18/8/X5

Supplier
Beacon Ltd

Filing cabinets: Grey 4 @ £150.00
Filing cabinets: Cream 2 @ £150.00
Discount: 20%

J Tarvey

WORKBASE OFFICE SUPPLIES LTD
63 Conduit Street
Liverpool L1 6NN

PURCHASE ORDER
P07338

16/8/X5

Supplier
Weston Suppliers

Ballpoints - black (50s) × 100
Ballpoints - blue (50s) × 100
Both at £3.00 per 50
Discount 10%

J Tarvey

WORKBASE OFFICE SUPPLIES LTD
63 Conduit Street
Liverpool L1 6NN

PURCHASE ORDER
P07345

20/8/X5

Supplier
Ryemead Ltd

Filing trays - Smoke 20 @ £8.50
 - Grey 10 @ £8.50
 - Slate blue 5 @ £8.50

J Tarvey

Trial run devolved assessments

WORKBASE OFFICE SUPPLIES LTD

63 Conduit Street
Liverpool L1 6NN

PURCHASE ORDER
P07348

20/8/X5

Supplier
Harbord Ltd

Typist's chair - Paprika
5 @ £95.00
Discount 15%

J Tarvey

WORKBASE OFFICE SUPPLIES LTD

63 Conduit Street
Liverpool L1 6NN

GOODS RECEIVED NOTE
GRN4168

28/8/X5

Supplier
Kineton Ltd

Cardboard Packaging - 100kg

Received in good condition	GL
Short/ Damaged	

WORKBASE OFFICE SUPPLIES LTD

63 Conduit Street
Liverpool L1 6NN

GOODS RECEIVED NOTE
GRN4172

27/8/X5

Supplier
Beacon Ltd

Grey filing cabinets × 3
Cream filing cabinets × 2

Received in good condition	
Short/ Damaged	1 Grey filing cabinet badly dented - sent back

---

WORKBASE OFFICE SUPPLIES LTD

63 Conduit Street
Liverpool L1 6NN

GOODS RECEIVED NOTE
GRN4179

27/8/X5

Supplier
Weston Supplies

Ballpoints - Blue (50s) × 100
Ballpoints - Black (50s) × 100

Received in good condition	GL
Short/ Damaged	

WORKBASE OFFICE SUPPLIES LTD

63 Conduit Street
Liverpool L1 6NN

GOODS RECEIVED NOTE
GRN4170
26/8/X5

Supplier
Ryemead Ltd

Filing trays - smoke × 20
- slate blue × 5
- grey × 10

Received in good condition	GL
Short/Damaged	

WORKBASE OFFICE SUPPLIES LTD

63 Conduit Street
Liverpool L1 6NN

GOODS RECEIVED NOTE
GRN4169
26/8/X5

Supplier
Harbord Ltd

Typist's chairs - Paprika × 5

Received in good condition	GL
Short/Damaged	

WORKBASE OFFICE SUPPLIES LTD
MEMORANDUM

TASK 3

At 31 August 20X5:

(a) the list of balances in the sales ledger totalled £11,622.42 DR and
(b) the list of balances in the purchase ledger totalled £7,244.05 CR.

At the same date, the balances on the control accounts were as follows.

Sales ledger control	£11,760.37	DR
Purchase ledger control	£7,742.20	CR

The following items are also relevant.

(i) Contra entries are to be made between Kineton Ltd's sales ledger account (code K022) and the company's purchase ledger account (code 021K) for £82.00.

(ii) The debit balance of £39.44 on Beacon Ltd's purchase ledger account (code 033B) is to be set off in full against the balance on a second purchase ledger account (code 042B) for the same supplier.

(iii) A single cash receipt of £610.00 from Conduit Insurance Co plc was correctly posted to Conduit's sales ledger account, but was incorrectly posted to the purchase ledger control account instead of the sales ledger control account.

(iv) The total of an invoice from Weston Supplies for £197.40, which was part of a batch of invoices which were correctly posted to the main ledger, was incorrectly posted as £179.40 including VAT to the supplier's account (code 041W).

(v) An invoice for £472.05 from Ryemead Ltd was correctly posted to the supplier's purchase ledger account (code 071R), but was posted to the sales ledger control account in error, instead of the purchase ledger control account.

(vi) The balance of £342.20 on the account of a supplier, Harbord Ltd (code 700H) was omitted from the totalling of the purchase ledger accounts.

You are required to write journal entries for the above items, or detail what other action is necessary.

TRIAL RUN DEVOLVED ASSESSMENT 5
PAPER PRODUCTS

FOUNDATION STAGE - NVQ/SVQ2

Unit 2

Making and Recording Payments

The purpose of this Trial Run Devolved Assessment is to give you an idea of what an AAT simulation looks like. It is not intended as a definitive guide to the tasks you may be required to perform.

The suggested time allowance for this Assessment is **one and a half hours**. Up to 30 minutes extra time may be permitted in an AAT simulation. Breaks in assessment will be allowed in the AAT simulation, but it must normally be completed in one day.

Calculators may be used but no reference material is permitted.

DO NOT OPEN THIS PAPER UNTIL YOU ARE READY TO START UNDER TIMED CONDITIONS

Trial run devolved assessments

INSTRUCTIONS

This Assessment is designed to test your ability to record and account for credit transactions.

The situation is provided on Page 151.

You are provided with data on Pages 153-157 which you must use to complete the related tasks on Page 152.

Your answers should be set out in this booklet using the documents provided. You may require additional answer pages.

You are allowed one and a half hours to complete your work.

A high level of accuracy is required. Check your work carefully.

Correcting fluid may be used, but should be used in moderation. Errors should be crossed out neatly and clearly. You should write in black ink, not pencil.

You are advised to read the whole of the Assessment before commencing as all of the information may be of value and is not necessarily supplied in the sequence in which you might wish to deal with it.

A full suggested solution to this Assessment is provided on Page 247 of this Kit.

THE SITUATION

Your name is Alison Greenwood and you are the bookkeeper for Paper Products Ltd, 139 Garstang Road, Preston PR1 8HG.

It is Friday 30 May 20X7.

The business is a wholesaler and mail order supplier of stationery products. It now sells a wide variety of stationery products by mail order and to stationery suppliers and retailers and has a sales team which covers the whole country.

The business is registered for Value Added Tax.

Your duties as bookkeeper include the following.

(a) Establishing the necessary bookkeeping entries and opening up the necessary accounts for new suppliers.

(b) Once accounts have been established for new suppliers, you are responsible for posting the invoices to the suppliers accounts in the purchase ledger and the purchases account and the VAT account in the main ledger.

(c) Posting purchases to the creditors account.

Trial run devolved assessments

THE TASKS TO BE PERFORMED

Blank documents on page(s)

1 Enter the new supplier details into the purchases day book, enter the invoices and total up at the end of the month ensuring that the day book balances. — 153

2 Open accounts for each of the new suppliers and post the invoices to the suppliers accounts in the purchases ledger, carrying down the balances at the month end. — 154 - 156

3 Post the totals of the new suppliers accounts to the purchases account and VAT account in the main (nominal) ledger. — 156

4 Post the totals to the creditors account in the main ledger to complete the double entry. — 157

Note. VAT should be rounded up or down to the nearest penny.

5: Paper Products (data, tasks and answer booklet)

DATA

New suppliers for May 20X7

Date	Supplier	Goods £	VAT £	Total £
8 May	Murray Bros	741.30	129.73	871.03
9 May	Johnson & Co	142.00	24.85	166.85
14 May	Drury & Brown	407.50	71.31	478.81
17 May	Lever Bros	86.30	15.10	101.40
18 May	Bell and Davies	107.58	18.83	126.41
20 May	Lancs CC	1,110.48	194.33	1,304.81
22 May	John Dawson	15.97	2.79	18.76
22 May	The Paper Shop	222.20	38.89	261.09
26 May	Sams Supplies	346.47	60.63	407.10
27 May	Speakman Products	115.99	20.30	136.29

PURCHASES DAY BOOK

Date	Details	Goods £	VAT £	Total £

PURCHASE LEDGER

	£		£

	£		£

	£		£

	£		£

5: Paper Products (data, tasks and answer booklet)

	£		£

	£		£

	£		£

	£		£

Trial run devolved assessments

	£		£

	£		£

MAIN (NOMINAL) LEDGER
PURCHASES ACCOUNT

	£		£

VAT ACCOUNT

	£		£

CREDITORS CONTROL ACCOUNT

	£		£

TRIAL RUN DEVOLVED ASSESSMENT 6
CATERING CONTRACTS

FOUNDATION STAGE - NVQ/SVQ2

Unit 2

Making and Recording Payements

The purpose of this Trial Run Devolved Assessment is to give you an idea of what an AAT simulation looks like. It is not intended as a definitive guide to the tasks you may be required to perform.

The suggested time allowance for this Assessment is **one and a half hours**. Up to 30 minutes extra time may be permitted in an AAT simulation. Breaks in assessment will be allowed in the AAT simulation, but it must normally be completed in one day.

Calculators may be used but no reference material is permitted.

DO NOT OPEN THIS PAPER UNTIL YOU ARE READY TO START UNDER TIMED CONDITIONS

Trial run devolved assessments

INSTRUCTIONS

This Assessment is designed to test your ability to record and account for credit transactions.

The situation is provided on Page 161.

You are provided with data on Page 163 which you must use to complete the related tasks on Page 162.

Your answers should be set out on Pages 164-168 using the documents provided. You may require additional answer pages.

You are allowed one and a half hours to complete your work.

A high level of accuracy is required. Check your work carefully.

Correcting fluid may be used but should be used in moderation. Errors should be crossed out neatly and clearly. You should write in black ink, not pencil.

You are advised to read the whole of the Assessment before commencing as all of the information may be of value and is not necessarily supplied in the sequence in which you might wish to deal with it.

A full suggested solution to this Assessment is provided on Page 251 of this Kit.

THE SITUATION

Your name is Derek Oldfield and you are employed as the bookkeeper for Catering Contacts Ltd, an organisation which specialises in the supply of catering equipment to the catering industry.

The address of Catering Contacts Ltd is 75, Parr Street, Kendal, Cumbria LA9 5HE and today's date is Friday 27th June 20X7.

The business is registered for Value Added Tax and its products are bought and sold at a standard rate of 17.5%.

Your duties include the following.

(a) Drawing up the purchases day book.
(b) Posting invoices to the suppliers' accounts in the purchase ledger.
(c) Posting total invoices to the relevant accounts in the general (main) ledger.

THE TASKS TO BE PERFORMED

Blank document on page(s)

1 Draw up the purchases day book, for the purchase invoices received during June, enter the invoices and total up at the end of the month ensuring that the day book balances.   164

2 Open accounts for each of the suppliers and post the invoices to the suppliers' accounts in the purchase ledger. Balance off the suppliers' accounts and carry forward the balances.   165-167

3 Post the total invoices to the purchase and VAT account in the general ledger and the creditors account. Balance off these accounts and carry forward the balances.   167-168

4 List the outstanding creditors at the end of June.   168

Note. VAT should be rounded up or down to the nearest penny.

DATA

Purchase invoices received for June

Date	Supplier	Goods £	VAT £	Total £
6 June	Thomas Hardy	74.80		
7 June	Ealing & Co	176.95		
11 June	Bryant Associates	243.44		
14 June	Clark and Robinson	98.56		
14 June	Bass Ltd	346.58		
17 June	J Adams Ltd	106.00		
21 June	W Larkin	37.59		
23 June	J Bryers Ltd	179.56		
24 June	A Stewart & Co	274.07		
26 June	M Ealham Ltd	659.86		

Note. VAT and the total invoice value have not yet been calculated.

PURCHASES DAY BOOK

Date	Details	Goods £	VAT £	Total £

6: Catering Contracts (data, tasks and answer booklet)

PURCHASES LEDGER

	£		£

	£		£

	£		£

	£		£

PURCHASES LEDGER

Trial run devolved assessments

	£		£

	£		£

MAIN LEDGER

PURCHASES ACCOUNT

	£		£

VAT ACCOUNT

	£		£

CREDITORS CONTROL ACCOUNT

	£		£

Outstanding creditors at the end of June

Solutions to practice devolved assessments

1: Powell Cars

SOLUTION TO PRACTICE DEVOLVED ASSESSMENT 1: POWELL CARS

Tutorial note. Petty cash transactions are usually quite straightforward as long as the proper procedures and rules are followed. These will vary from organisation to organisation, but generally, the important points are:

(a) to use petty cash *only* for suitable transactions; and
(b) to obtain the correct authorisation(s).

You should also note that, in this assignment, IOUs in petty cash must be paid back *before* the monthly petty cash count and imprest top-up.

Extracting VAT from payments is practised here. You should know about the VAT-rating of usual business expenses.

Solution

(a) It would not be appropriate to pay the invoice from Wright's Garage through petty cash. It exceeds the £100 limit and it is not in the nature of a normal petty cash transaction. M Smythe should obtain reimbursement through staff expenses or through normal purchase/expense payments procedures.

Assuming that office procedures have been followed, the IOU from J. Smith dated 15/4/X5 should have been repaid before the petty cash count at the end of April 20X5. Therefore this transaction can be ignored.

Note. To extract VAT from a gross figure, multiply the figure by $7/47$ ($17.5/117.5$).

Petty cash vouchers have been prepared for the other transactions as follows.

No 1563		
Petty Cash Voucher		
Date 3/4/X5		
	AMOUNT	
	£	p
Office cleaner	15	00
	15	00
Signature: M Jones		
Authorised by: G. Earle		

No 1564		
Petty Cash Voucher		
Date 3/4/X5		
	AMOUNT	
	£	p
Cowcream Dairy (milk)	9	75
	9	75
Signature: P Clark		
Authorised by: G. Earle		

Solutions to practice devolved assessments

Petty Cash Voucher No 1565
Date 6/4/X5

	AMOUNT	
	£	p
Cash received for stamps	1	62
	1	62

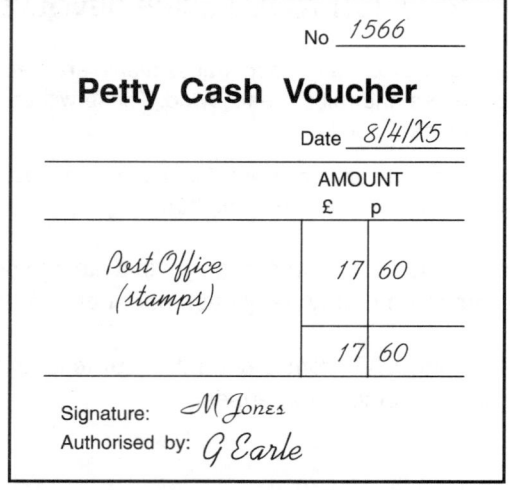

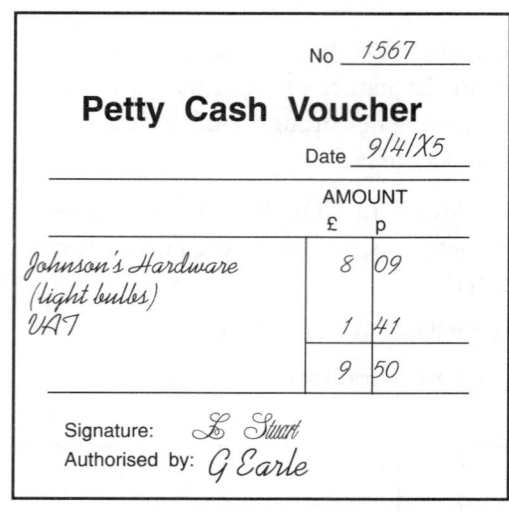

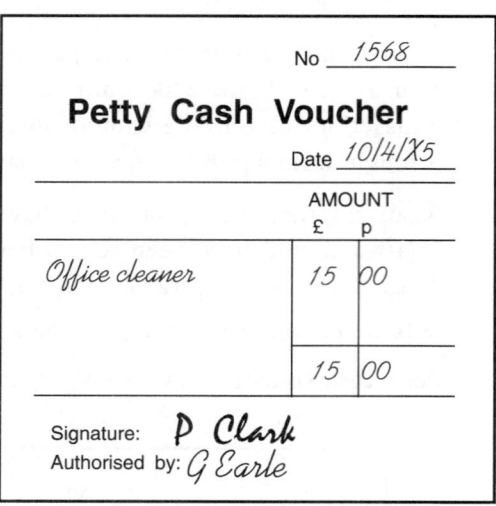

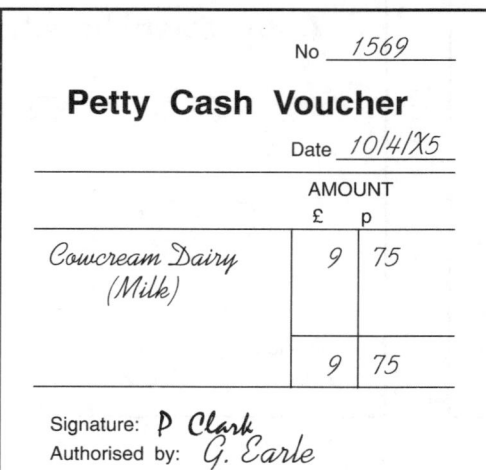

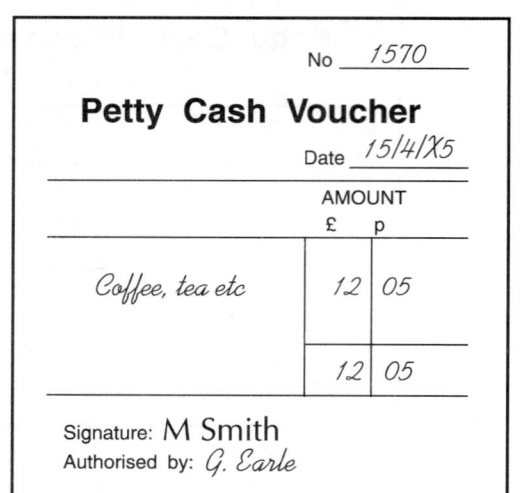

Signature: C Chappell
Authorised by: G Earle

Petty Cash Voucher No 1566
Date 8/4/X5

	AMOUNT	
	£	p
Post Office (stamps)	17	60
	17	60

Signature: M Jones
Authorised by: G Earle

Petty Cash Voucher No 1567
Date 9/4/X5

	AMOUNT	
	£	p
Johnson's Hardware (light bulbs)	8	09
VAT	1	41
	9	50

Signature: L Stuart
Authorised by: G Earle

Petty Cash Voucher No 1568
Date 10/4/X5

	AMOUNT	
	£	p
Office cleaner	15	00
	15	00

Signature: P Clark
Authorised by: G Earle

Petty Cash Voucher No 1569
Date 10/4/X5

	AMOUNT	
	£	p
Cowcream Dairy (Milk)	9	75
	9	75

Signature: P Clark
Authorised by: G Earle

Petty Cash Voucher No 1570
Date 15/4/X5

	AMOUNT	
	£	p
Coffee, tea etc	12	05
	12	05

Signature: M Smith
Authorised by: G. Earle

1: Powell Cars

No 1571
Petty Cash Voucher
Date 17/4/X5

	AMOUNT	
	£	p
Office cleaner	15	00
	15	00

Signature: P Clark
Authorised by: G Earle

No 1572
Petty Cash Voucher
Date 17/4/X5

	AMOUNT	
	£	p
Cowcream Dairy (milk)	9	75
	9	75

Signature: P Clark
Authorised by: G Earle

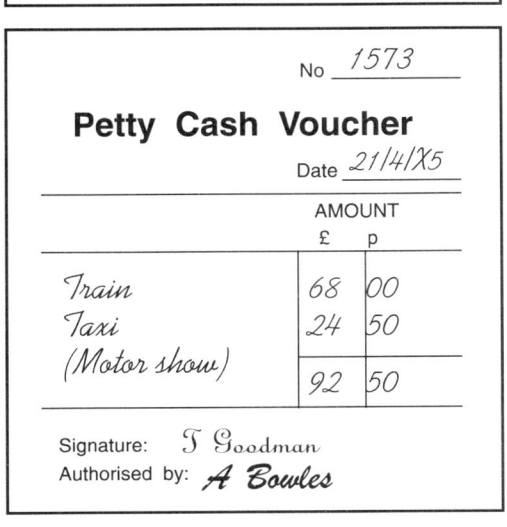

No 1573
Petty Cash Voucher
Date 21/4/X5

	AMOUNT	
	£	p
Train	68	00
Taxi (Motor show)	24	50
	92	50

Signature: T Goodman
Authorised by: A Bowles

No 1574
Petty Cash Voucher
Date 21/4/X5

	AMOUNT	
	£	p
Train	68	00
Taxi (motor show)	18	30
	86	30

Signature: C Chappell
Authorised by: A Bowles

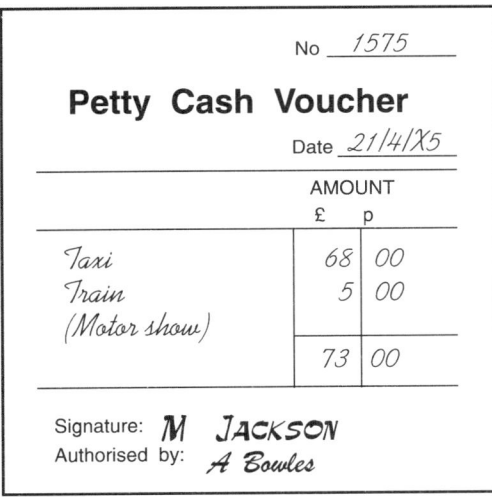

No 1575
Petty Cash Voucher
Date 21/4/X5

	AMOUNT	
	£	p
Taxi	68	00
Train (Motor show)	5	00
	73	00

Signature: M JACKSON
Authorised by: A Bowles

No 1576
Petty Cash Voucher
Date 22/4/X5

	AMOUNT	
	£	p
Johnson's Hardware (cleaning materials)	26	06
VAT	4	56
	30	62

Signature: P Clark
Authorised by: A Smeed

Solutions to practice devolved assessments

Petty Cash Voucher No 1577
Date 24/4/X5

	AMOUNT	
	£	p
Subsistence (Bentil's Wine Bar)	44	92
VAT	7	86
	52	78

Signature: C Chappell **P Simpson**
Authorised by: **A Smeed**

Petty Cash Voucher No 1578
Date 24/4/X5

	AMOUNT	
	£	p
Office cleaner	15	00
	15	00

Signature: M Jones
Authorised by: G Earle

Petty Cash Voucher No 1579
Date 24/4/X5

	AMOUNT	
	£	p
Cowcream Dairy (milk)	7	80
	7	80

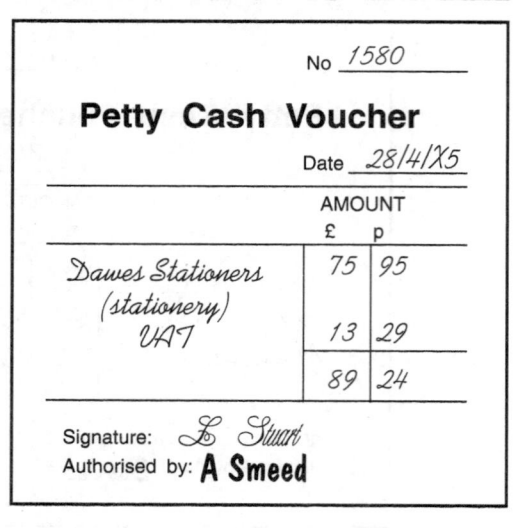

Signature: P Clark
Authorised by: G Earle

Petty Cash Voucher No 1580
Date 28/4/X5

	AMOUNT	
	£	p
Dawes Stationers (stationery)	75	95
VAT	13	29
	89	24

Signature: L Stuart
Authorised by: **A Smeed**

1: Powell Cars

(b) Petty cash book

PETTY CASH BOOK

Details	Net receipt £	VAT £	Total £	Date	Details	Voucher No	Total £	Travel £	Postage & stationery £	Staff welfare £	Office supplies £	Sundry £	VAT £
Balance b/f			1,000.00	3.4	Office Cleaner	1563	15.00					15.00	
Cash received (stamps)	1.62		1.62	3.4	Cowcream Dairy	1564	9.75			9.75			
				6.4		1565							
				8.4	Post Office	1566	17.60		17.60				
				9.4	Johnson's Hardware	1567	9.50				8.09		1.41
				10.4	Office Cleaner	1568	15.00					15.00	
				10.4	Cowcream Dairy	1569	9.75			9.75			
				15.4	Coffee etc	1570	12.05			12.05			
				17.4	Office Cleaner	1571	15.00					15.00	
				17.4	Cowcream Dairy	1572	9.75			9.75			
				21.4	T Goodman	1573	92.50	92.50					
				21.4	C Chappell	1574	86.30	86.30					
				21.4	M Jackson	1575	73.00	73.00					
				22.4	Johnson's Hardware	1576	30.62				26.06		4.56
				24.4	Subsistence	1577	52.78			44.92			7.86
				24.4	Office Cleaner	1578	15.00					15.00	
				24.4	Cowcream Dairy	1579	7.80			7.80			
				28.4	Dawes Stationers	1580	89.24				75.95		13.29
							560.64	251.80	17.60	94.02	110.10	60.00	27.12
				30.4	Write off difference		4.13					4.13	
					Balance c/d		1,000.00					64.13	
	1.62		563.15				1,564.77						
			1564.77										
Cash book													

175

Solutions to practice devolved assessments

(c) Petty cash reconciliation

	£
Notes and coin (W1)	436.85
Vouchers for payments (W2)	560.64
Vouchers for receipts	(1.62)
	995.87
Difference	4.13
Imprest amount	1,000.00

Workings

1   *Notes and coin*

		£
£20 × 11		220.00
£10 × 10		100.00
£5 × 12		60.00
£1 × 37		37.00
50p × 23		11.50
20p × 33		6.60
10p × 12		1.20
5p × 9		0.45
2p × 4		0.08
1p × 2		0.02
		436.85

2   *Petty cash vouchers: payments*

No.	£
1563	15.00
1564	9.75
1566	17.60
1567	9.50
1568	15.00
1569	9.75
1570	12.05
1571	15.00
1572	9.75
1573	92.50
1574	86.30
1575	73.00
1576	30.62
1577	52.78
1578	15.00
1579	7.80
1580	89.24
	560.64

The difference on the petty cash reconciliation shows a shortfall of £4.13. This could have arisen for a variety of reasons.

(i) Someone may have taken some petty cash but forgotten to put in a receipt or invoice and hence no voucher will have been completed.

(ii) Someone may have borrowed the cash and forgotten to put in an IOU.

(iii) The money may have been stolen.

The action taken over the discrepancy will depend on company rules and procedures. If all differences less than, say £10, can be written off and ignored, then no further investigation is necessary. If, however, the company rules state that all differences should be investigated, then the petty cashier and/or the office supervisor will be obliged to make enquiries to discover the cause of the difference. If no cause is found, then presumably the difference can be written off.

1: Powell Cars

If shortfalls continue on a regular basis, then security procedures surrounding petty cash should be reviewed.

(d) The cash necessary to top up the imprest amount will be:

	£
Imprest amount	1,000.00
Less cash in till	436.85
Cheque required	563.15

The cash required *could* be made up as follows.

			£
£20	×	7	140.00
£10	×	23	230.00
£5	×	20	100.00
£1	×	50	50.00
50p	×	40	20.00
20p	×	50	10.00
10p	×	100	10.00
5p	×	40	2.00
2p	×	25	0.50
1p	×	65	0.65
			563.15

Cheque Requisition   247323

Date: 30 April 20X5
Payable to: Cash
Amount: £563.15
Details: Petty cash imprest April
Signed: G Earle   A Bowles

Southern Bank   30/4   20 X5

17 CHISWICK HIGH ROAD, LONDON W4 6EG

11-21-33
SOUTHERN BANK PLC

or order

Pay Cash
Five hundred and sixty-three pounds 15p

£ 563.15

PER PRO
POWELLS LIMITED

Cheque No.   Branch No.   Account No.

⑈101129⑈ ⑆21-33⑆ 19274882⑈

Solutions to practice devolved assessments

(e) The petty cash transactions would be posted as follows.

Account name	Account code	Debit £	Credit £
Petty cash	2000	1.62	*564.77
Travel	1315	251.80	
Print, post and stationery	1205	17.60	
Staff welfare	1290	94.02	
Office supplies	1340	110.10	
Sundry	1395	64.13	
VAT	7000	27.12	
Sundry income	3400		1.62
		566.39	566.39

* £560.64 + £4.13

2: Ives

SOLUTION TO PRACTICE DEVOLVED ASSESSMENT 2: IVES

Tutorial note. This is quite a long assignment but it brings together all the aspects of making and recording payments. You will get some practice of calculating settlement discounts and there is an emphasis on obtaining the correct authorisation for payments. Controls over payments are very important as any weakness in this area can easily allow a fraud to take place.

You should note that the analysis and VAT columns should not be used for payments to creditors, since analysis has already taken place in the purchase day book. However, the sundry invoices must be analysed and the VAT split out in the cash book, as this has not been recorded elsewhere. Note also that VAT on motor cars is not reclaimable.

Solution

(a) (i) *Payments schedule*

Supplier	Gross amount £		Discount claimed £	Net amount £
Barton Bulk Paper (W1)	1,085.09	(3%)	32.55	1,052.54
Drips Industrial Dyes	530.20		-	530.20
Mache Paper plc (W2)	8,564.85	(2½%)	214.12	8,350.73
Rainbow Dyes	1,164.50		-	1,164.50
Wright Wrappings	420.17		-	420.17
Linton Paper Co (W3)	28,914.98	(1½%)	433.72	28,481.26
Bright Dyes	2,058.00	(2%)	41.16	2,016.84
Prior Paper Products	3,194.78		-	3,194.78
Total due	45,932.57		721.55	45,211.02

Workings

1 *Barton Bulk Paper*

Amounts payable per statement			£
Invoice	117649		461.61
Invoice	117668		917.11
Credit note	424492		(165.81)
			1,212.91
Less credit outstanding			(127.82)
			1,085.09

2 *Mache Paper plc*

Amounts payable per statement			£
Invoice	4274842		3,091.12
Invoice	4275204		1,584.47
Invoice	4275432		4,217.14
Credit note	5881729		(327.88)
			8,564.85

3 *Linton Paper Co*

Amounts payable per statement			£
Invoice	10736509		3,721.59
Invoice	10736615		2,632.56
Invoice	10736692		7,789.17
Invoice	10737047		4,824.96
Invoice	10737222		2,167.85
Invoice	10737514		7,778.85
			28,914.98

Solutions to practice devolved assessments

(ii) *Remittance advices*

14723

REMITTANCE ADVICE

TO: Barton Bulk Paper
10 June Street
Barnsley, Yorkshire   J6676

IVES PLC
Works Lane
Walsall
01922 42731

| Account Ref | B001 | Date | 29/5/X5 | Page | 1 |

DATE	DETAILS	INVOICES	CREDIT NOTES	PAYMENT AMOUNT
26.5.X5	Invoice 117649	461.61		461.61
27.5.X5	Invoice 117668	917.11		917.11
29.5.X5	Credit note 424492		165.81	-165.81
29.5.X5	Credit outstanding		127.82	-127.82
29.5.X5	Discount at 3%		32.55	-32.55
	Total	1,378.72	326.18	1052.54

14724

REMITTANCE ADVICE

TO: Drips Industrial Dyes
44 Wain Estate
Walsall   117428

IVES PLC
Works Lane
Walsall
01922 42731

| Account Ref | D001 | Date | 29/5/X5 | Page | 1 |

DATE	DETAILS	INVOICES	CREDIT NOTES	PAYMENT AMOUNT
1.5.X5	Invoice S42738	53.50		53.50
2.5.X5	Invoice S42742	30.90		30.90
6.5.X5	Invoice S42783	30.90		30.90
8.5.X5	Credit note C42801		22.60	-22.60
10.5.X5	Invoice S42829	92.70		92.70
14.5.X5	Invoice S42856	56.60		56.60
21.5.X5	Invoice S42911	30.90		30.90
23.5.X5	Invoice S42934	56.60		56.60
	Carried forward	352.10	22.60	329.50

14725

REMITTANCE ADVICE

IVES PLC
Works Lane
Walsall
01922 42731

TO: Drips Industrial Dyes
44 Wain Estate
Walsall   117428

Account Ref: D001   Date: 29/5/X5   Page: 2

DATE	DETAILS	INVOICES	CREDIT NOTES	PAYMENT AMOUNT
24.5.X5	Brought forward	352.10	22.60	329.50
29.5.X5	Invoice S42940	113.20		113.50
	Invoice S42971	87.50		87.50
	Total	552.80	22.60	530.20

14726

REMITTANCE ADVICE

IVES PLC
Works Lane
Walsall
01922 42731

TO: Mache Paper PLC
Black Country Trading Estate
Birmingham   173271

Account Ref: M001   Date: 29/5/X5   Page: 1

DATE	DETAILS	INVOICES	CREDIT NOTES	PAYMENT AMOUNT
15.5.X5	Invoice 4274842	3,091.12		3,091.12
20.5.X5	Invoice 4275204	1,584.47		1,584.47
27.5.X5	Invoice 4275432	4,217.14		4,217.14
28.5.X5	Credit note 5881729		327.88	-327.88
29.5.X5	Discount at 2.5%		214.12	-214.12
	Total	8,892.73	542.00	8,350.73

14727

REMITTANCE ADVICE

TO: Rainbow Dyes Ltd
14 Rothside Road
Birmingham   J4217

IVES PLC
Works Lane
Walsall
01922 42731

| Account Ref | R001 | Date | 29/5/X5 | Page | 1 |

DATE	DETAILS	INVOICES	CREDIT NOTES	PAYMENT AMOUNT
1.5.X5	Invoice 401136	137.00		137.00
5.5.X5	Invoice 401192	171.25		171.25
7.5.X5	Invoice 401235	102.75		102.75
14.5.X5	Credit note C6374		68.50	-68.50
15.5.X5	Invoice 401317	274.00		274.00
19.5.X5	Invoice 401389	102.75		102.75
22.5.X5	Invoice 401442	137.00		137.00
26.5.X5	Invoice 401470	239.75		239.75
	Carried forward	1,164.50	68.50	1,096.00

14728

REMITTANCE ADVICE

TO: Rainbow Dyes Ltd
14, Rothside Road
Birmingham   J4217

IVES PLC
Works Lane
Walsall
01922 42731

| Account Ref | R001 | Date | 29/5/X5 | Page | 2 |

DATE	DETAILS	INVOICES	CREDIT NOTES	PAYMENT AMOUNT
	Brought forward	1,164.50	68.50	1,096.00
28.5.X5	Credit note C6428		102.75	-102.75
28.5.X5	Invoice 401522	171.25		171.25
	Total	1,335.75	171.25	1,164.50

14729

REMITTANCE ADVICE

TO: Wright Wrappings
34 George's Yard
Manchester J042

IVES PLC
Works Lane
Walsall
01922 42731

| Account Ref | W001 | Date | 29/5/X5 | Page | 1 |

DATE	DETAILS	INVOICES	CREDIT NOTES	PAYMENT AMOUNT
1.5.X5	Invoice 12423	127.52		127.52
13.5.X5	Invoice 12451	141.80		141.80
20.5.X5	Invoice 12493	92.63		92.63
25.5.X5	Invoice 12520	58.22		58.22
	Total	420.17		420.17

14730

REMITTANCE ADVICE

TO: Linton Paper Co
Kemp Trading Estate
Birmingham J1234

IVES PLC
Works Lane
Walsall
01922 42731

| Account Ref | L001 | Date | 29/5/X5 | Page | 1 |

DATE	DETAILS	INVOICES	CREDIT NOTES	PAYMENT AMOUNT
18.5.X5	Invoice 10736509	3,721.59		3,721.59
20.5.X5	Invoice 10736615	2,632.56		2,632.56
21.5.X5	Invoice 10736692	7,789.17		7,789.17
25.5.X5	Invoice	4,824.96		4,824.96
27.5.X5	Invoice	2,167.85		2,167.85
28.5.X5	Invoice	7,778.85		7,778.85
29.5.X5	Discount at 1.5%		433.72	-433.72
		28,914.98	433.72	28,481.26

Solutions to practice devolved assessments

```
14731
```

REMITTANCE ADVICE

TO: Bright Dyes Ltd
4 37 Tilley Hill
Newcastle-upon-Tyne   432117

IVES PLC
Works Lane
Walsall
01922 42731

Account Ref: B002   Date: 29/5/X5   Page: 1

DATE	DETAILS	INVOICES	CREDIT NOTES	PAYMENT AMOUNT
17.5.X5	Invoice IN143517	740.88		740.88
18.5.X5	Invoice IN143642	246.96		246.96
21.5.X5	Invoice IN143739	329.28		329.28
25.5.X5	Invoice IN143890	164.64		164.64
26.5.X5	Invoice IN143944	82.32		82.32
28.5.X5	Invoice IN144086	493.92		493.92
	Discount at 2%		41.16	-41.16
	Total	2,058.00	41.16	2,016.84

```
14732
```

REMITTANCE ADVICE

TO: Prior Paper Products Ltd
4 Berry Street
Liverpool   01179

IVES PLC
Works Lane
Walsall
01922 42731

Account Ref: P001   Date: 29/5/X5   Page: 1

DATE	DETAILS	INVOICES	CREDIT NOTES	PAYMENT AMOUNT
2.4.X5	Invoice J1724057	393.95		393.95
6.4.X5	Invoice J1724322	482.96		482.96
8.4.X5	Invoice J1724509	120.78		120.78
15.4.X5	Credit note (inv. J1723112)		28.70	-28.70
17.4.X5	Invoice J1724814	261.61		261.61
22.4.X5	Invoice J1725072	167.04		167.04
24.4.X5	Invoice J1725159	209.81		209.81
28.4.X5	Credit note (inv. J1724322)		68.57	-68.57
	Carried forward	1,636.15	97.27	1,538.88

14733				
REMITTANCE ADVICE			IVES PLC	
			Works Lane	
TO: Prior Paper Products Ltd			Walsall	
4 Berry Street			01922 42731	
Liverpool 0117 9				

Account Ref	P001	Date	29/5/X5	Page	2

DATE	DETAILS	INVOICES	CREDIT NOTES	PAYMENT AMOUNT
	Brought forward	1,636.15	97.27	1,538.88
1.5.X5	Invoice J1725380	380.65		380.65
6.5.X5	Invoice J1725442	377.67		377.67
8.5.X5	Invoice J1725589	631.52		631.52
12.5.X5	Invoice J1725710	70.15		70.15
15.5.X5	Invoice J1725846	194.77		194.77
19.5.X5	Invoice J1725994	108.49		108.49
25.5.X5	Credit note (inv. J1724322)		49.84	-49.84
26.5.X5	Credit note (inv. J1725589)		57.51	-57.51
		3,399.40	204.62	3,194.78

(b) (i) D Hill: the expenses claim form can be authorised by the sales director or the finance manager. Only one signature is needed.

C Prior: the total has been overcast by £50. The totals should be:

Net	VAT	Total
£	£	£
182.27	21.59	203.86

Supporting documentation required for these and the other expenses claim forms would comprise the following.

(1) VAT invoices for petrol, repairs and service, telephone bills and restaurant bills

(2) Receipts for parking, taxis and car tax

(3) Train tickets (or equivalent receipts)

(ii) Cheque requisition forms

```
                                                        247320
              Cheque Requisition

    Date        29 May 20X5
    Payable to  Mr D Hill
    Amount      £393.95
    Details     Expenses for May


    Signed      S Smith
```

```
                                                        247321
              Cheque Requisition

    Date        29 May 20X5
    Payable to  Mr R Chalmers
    Amount      £395.29
    Details     Expenses for May


    Signed      S Smith
```

```
                                                        247322
              Cheque Requisition

    Date        29 May 20X5
    Payable to  Ms L Graves
    Amount      £360.62
    Details     Expenses for May


    Signed      S Smith
```

```
                                                              247323
                    Cheque Requisition

    Date        29 May 20X5
    Payable to  Mr C Prior
    Amount      £203.86
    Details     Expenses for May


    Signed      S Smith
```

```
                                                              247324
                    Cheque Requisition

    Date        29 May 20X5
    Payable to  Mr J Clark
    Amount      £196.22
    Details     Expenses for May


    Signed      S Smith
```

(c) Authorisation for the invoices should be obtained as follows.

Speedy Transport Ltd: T Jones, Sales Director
Johnson's Plastic Products: R Banner, Purchasing Director
Dawes Stationery: S Smith, Finance Manager
Office Supplies Ltd: S Chapman, Finance Director

14734

REMITTANCE ADVICE

TO: Speedy Transport Ltd
42, Belman's Yard
Liverpool

IVES PLC
Works Lane
Walsall
01922 42731

Account Ref: —   Date: 29/5/X5   Page: 1

DATE	DETAILS	INVOICES	CREDIT NOTES	PAYMENT AMOUNT
22.5.X5	Invoice 174827	1,729.60		1,729.60
	Total	1,729.60		1,729.60

14735

REMITTANCE ADVICE

TO: Johnson's Plastic Products
302 Birbeck Estate
Birmingham

IVES PLC
Works Lane
Walsall
01922 42731

Account Ref: —   Date: 29/5/X5   Page: 1

DATE	DETAILS	INVOICES	CREDIT NOTES	PAYMENT AMOUNT
20.5.X5	Invoice 42767	781.85		781.85
	Total	781.85		781.85

14736

REMITTANCE ADVICE

TO: Dawes Stationery
297 Hillside Road
Walsall

IVES PLC
Works Lane
Walsall
01922 42731

| Account Ref | ✓ | Date | 29/5/X5 | Page | 1 |

DATE	DETAILS	INVOICES	CREDIT NOTES	PAYMENT AMOUNT
28.5.X5	Invoice 1728	120.97		120.97
	Total	120.97		120.97

14737

REMITTANCE ADVICE

TO: Office Supplies Ltd
1 Blackstone Way
Walsall

IVES PLC
Works Lane
Walsall
01922 42731

| Account Ref | ✓ | Date | 29/5/X5 | Page | 1 |

DATE	DETAILS	INVOICES	CREDIT NOTES	PAYMENT AMOUNT
21.5.X5	Invoice 27131	524.93		524.93
	Total	524.93		524.93

(d) Cheques

Northern Bank
17 BALSAM LANE, BIRMINGHAM BH 2SP

29 May 20 X5

20-27-48
NORTHERN BANK PLC

Pay Barton Bulk Paper   or order

One thousand and fifty – two pounds 54p   £ 1,052.54

Not negotiable

PER PRO IVES PLC

S Chapman

Cheque No.   Branch No.   Account No.

⑈101100⑈ 20⑈2748⑈ 30595713⑈

Northern Bank
17 BALSAM LANE, BIRMINGHAM BH 2SP

29 May 20 X5

20-27-48
NORTHERN BANK PLC

Pay Drips Industrial Dyes   or order

Five hundred and thirty pounds 20p   £ 530-20

Not negotiable

PER PRO IVES PLC

S Chapman

Cheque No.   Branch No.   Account No.

⑈101101⑈ 20⑈2748⑈ 30595713⑈

Northern Bank
17 BALSAM LANE, BIRMINGHAM BH 2SP

29 May 20 X5

20-27-48
NORTHERN BANK PLC

Pay Mache Paper plc   or order

Eight thousand three hundred and fifty pounds 73p –   £ 8,350.73

Not negotiable

PER PRO IVES PLC

S Chapman

Cheque No.   Branch No.   Account No.

⑈101102⑈ 20⑈2748⑈ 30595713⑈

Cheque 1

Northern Bank
17 BALSAM LANE, BIRMINGHAM BH 2SP

29 May 20 X5
20-27-48
NORTHERN BANK PLC

Pay Rainbow Dyes Ltd — or order

One thousand one hundred and sixty-four pounds 50p
Not negotiable

£ 1,164.50

PER PRO IVES PLC

S. Chapman

⑊101103⑊ 20⎯2748⑊ 30595713⑊

Cheque 2

Northern Bank
17 BALSAM LANE, BIRMINGHAM BH 2SP

29 May 20 X5
20-27-48
NORTHERN BANK PLC

Pay Wright Wrappings or order

Four hundred and twenty pounds 17p
Not negotiable

£ 420-17

PER PRO IVES PLC

S. Chapman

⑊101104⑊ 20⎯2748⑊ 30595713⑊

Cheque 3

Northern Bank
17 BALSAM LANE, BIRMINGHAM BH 2SP

29 May 20 X5
20-27-48
NORTHERN BANK PLC

Pay Linton Paper Co or order

Twenty-eight thousand four hundred and eighty one pounds 26p
Not negotiable

£ 28,481.26

PER PRO IVES PLC

S. Chapman
P. Hogwood

⑊101105⑊ 20⎯2748⑊ 30595713⑊

Solutions to practice devolved assessments

Northern Bank
17 BALSAM LANE, BIRMINGHAM BH 2SP

29 May 20 X5

20-27-48
NORTHERN BANK PLC

Pay Bright Dyes — or order

Two thousand and sixteen pounds 84p — Not negotiable

£ 2,016-84

PER PRO IVES PLC

S. Chapman

Cheque No. 101106 Branch No. 20-27-48 Account No. 30595713

Northern Bank
17 BALSAM LANE, BIRMINGHAM BH 2SP

29 May 20 X5

20-27-48
NORTHERN BANK PLC

Pay Prior Paper Products — or order

Three thousand one hundred and ninety-four pounds 78p — Not negotiable

£ 3,194.78

PER PRO IVES PLC

S Chapman

Cheque No. 101107 Branch No. 20-27-48 Account No. 30595713

Northern Bank
17 BALSAM LANE, BIRMINGHAM BH 2SP

29 May 20 X5

20-27-48
NORTHERN BANK PLC

Pay D. Hill — or order

Three hundred and ninety-three pounds 95p

£ 393-95

PER PRO IVES PLC

S Chapman

Cheque No. 101108 Branch No. 20-27-48 Account No. 30595713

Northern Bank
17 BALSAM LANE, BIRMINGHAM BH 2SP

29 May 20X5

20-27-48
NORTHERN BANK PLC

Pay R Chalmers   or order

Three hundred and ninety-five pounds 29p

£ 395.29

PER PRO IVES PLC

S Chapman

Cheque No.   Branch No.   Account No.

||"101109"|| 20"2748: 30595713"||

Northern Bank
17 BALSAM LANE, BIRMINGHAM BH 2SP

29 May 20X5

20-27-48
NORTHERN BANK PLC

Pay L. Graves   or order

Three hundred and sixty pounds 62p

£ 360-62

PER PRO IVES PLC

S Chapman

Cheque No.   Branch No.   Account No.

||"101110"|| 20"2748: 30595713"||

Northern Bank
17 BALSAM LANE, BIRMINGHAM BH 2SP

29 May 20X5

20-27-48
NORTHERN BANK PLC

Pay C. Prior   or order

Two hundred and three pounds 86p

£ 203.86

PER PRO IVES PLC

S Chapman

Cheque No.   Branch No.   Account No.

||"101111"|| 20"2748: 30595713"||

Northern Bank

17 BALSAM LANE, BIRMINGHAM BH 2SP

29 May 20 X5

20-27-48
NORTHERN BANK PLC

Pay J Clark   or order

One hundred and ninety-six pounds 22p

£ 196-22

PER PRO IVES PLC

S Chapman

⑈101112⑈ 20⑈2748⑆ 30595713⑈

Northern Bank

17 BALSAM LANE, BIRMINGHAM BH 2SP

29 May 20 X5

20-27-48
NORTHERN BANK PLC

Pay Speedy Transport Ltd   or order

One thousand seven hundred and twenty-nine pounds 60p

Not negotiable

£ 1,729.60

PER PRO IVES PLC

S Chapman

⑈101113⑈ 20⑈2748⑆ 30595713⑈

Northern Bank

17 BALSAM LANE, BIRMINGHAM BH 2SP

29 May 20 X5

20-27-48
NORTHERN BANK PLC

Pay Johnson's Plastic Products   or order

Seven hundred and eighty-one pounds 85p

Not negotiable

£ 781.85

PER PRO IVES PLC

S Chapman

⑈101114⑈ 20⑈27 8⑆ 30595713⑈

Northern Bank
17 BALSAM LANE, BIRMINGHAM BH 2SP

29 May 20 X5

20-27-48
NORTHERN BANK PLC

Pay Dawes Stationery   or order

One hundred and twenty pounds 97p   £ 120-97

Not negotiable

PER PRO IVES PLC

S Chapman

Cheque No.   Branch No.   Account No.

"101115" 20-2748: 30595713"

Northern Bank
17 BALSAM LANE, BIRMINGHAM BH 2SP

29 May 20 X5

20-27-48
NORTHERN BANK PLC

Pay Office Supplies Ltd   or order

Five hundred and twenty four pounds 93p   £ 524-93

Not negotiable

PER PRO IVES PLC

S Chapman

Cheque No.   Branch No.   Account No.

"101116" 20-2748: 30595713"

Solutions to practice devolved assessments

(e) (i) Standing order mandate

Standing Order Mandate

TO _Northern_ BANK

Address _17 Balsam Lane Birmingham BH 2SP_

	Bank	Branch Title (not address)	Sorting Code Number
Please pay	_Trust form_	_Birmingham_	_27-31-22_
	Beneficiary's Name		Account Number
for the credit of	_Flood and Fire_		_4117329_
	Regular amount in figures	Regular amount in words	
the sum of	£ _1,255.77_	_one thousand two hundred and fifty-five pounds and seventy-seven pence_	
	Date and Amount of First Payment	and thereafter every	Due Date and Frequency
commencing	_30 May 20X5_ £ _1,255.77_		_30th of each month_
	Date and Amount of Last Payment	*until you receive further notice from me/us in writing and debit my/our account accordingly.	
*until	_30 April 20X6_ £ _1,255.77_		
quoting the reference	_Insurance_		

This instruction cancels any previous order in favour of the beneficiary named above, under this reference.

Special instructions:

Account to be debited: _Ives plc_

Account Number: 3 0 5 9 5 7 1 3

Signature(s) _____

Date _29/5/X5_

*Delete if not applicable

(ii) Standing order payments are used by businesses and individuals to make regular payments of a fixed amount, for example paying the community charge or unified business rate by instalments. The *payer* must ask their bank to set up the standing order arrangement. The request will specify the amount to be paid, the frequency of payment and the name and bank details of the payee.

Direct debits, like standing orders, are used for regular payments. They differ from standing orders because it is the person who *receives* the payment who initiates each payment, and informs the bank of the amount of each payment. Another difference is that payments can be for a variable amount each time, and at irregular intervals, as well as for fixed amounts and at regular intervals. For example, direct debits might be used to pay a quarterly gas bill, which will vary in size each quarter.

(f) *Banker's draft request*

Application for Inland Draft
To Northern Bank Plc

Balsam Lane Branch   Date 29 May 20X5

Kindly supply a crossed Draft. *~~Marked 'account payee'~~

Payable to Plumy Motors LTD

£ 72,450.27 amount in words Seventy-two thousand, four hundred and fifty pounds 27p

*Please debit my/our account no | 3 | 0 | 5 | 9 | 5 | 7 | 1 | 3 |

*~~Herewith cash to cover~~

*~~Herewith cheque to cover~~

Charges (if any) to be ~~*deducted~~ / charged to me/us   Delete as necessary

Signature(s) P. Hogwood   S Chapman
Name(s)   P HOGWOOD   S CHAPMAN
Address   N/A
(if not a customer)

I/We acknowledge receipt of the above mentioned Draft numbered _____

_____ Signature

(To be signed by an authorised person in the company and returned to the bank)

Solutions to practice devolved assessments

(g) To stop the cheque I would telephone the bank immediately to request a stop and then I would write to confirm the instruction as follows.

IVES PLC
Works Lane
Walsall

The Manager
Northern Bank
17 Balsam Lane
Birmingham

DATE: 29 May 20X5

Dear Sir

ACCOUNT NO 30595713

We wish to confirm our request by telephone that the payment of the cheque detailed below is stopped.

Cheque No	101108
Dated	29 May 20X5
Amount £	393.95
Payee	D. Hill

We have inspected our statements up to number __254__ inclusive and the cheque is not listed on them.

We have drawn a replacement cheque number __N/A__.

Yours faithfully

(h) Cash book

MAY - PAYMENTS

	Date	Details	Cheque number	Discounts Received		Total		VAT		Creditors	
1	29.5.X5	Barton Bulk Paper	101100	32	55	1,052	54			1,052	54
2	"	Drips Industrial Dyes	101101			530	20			530	20
3	"	Mache Paper plc	101102	214	12	8,350	73			8,350	73
4	"	Rainbow Dyes	101103			1,164	50			1,164	50
5	"	Wright Wrappings	101104			420	17			420	17
6	"	Linton Paper Co.	101105	433	72	28,481	26			28,481	26
7	"	Bright Dyes	101106	41	16	2,016	84			2,016	84
8	"	Prior Paper Products	101107			3,194	78			3,194	78
9	"	~~D. Hill~~ CANCELLED	101108			~~393~~	~~95~~	~~56~~	~~48~~		
10	"	R Chalmers (expenses)	101109			395	29	54	15		
11	"	L Graves (expenses)	101110			360	62	42	30		
12	"	C Prior (expenses)	101111			203	86	21	59		
13	"	J Clark (expenses)	101112			196	22	25	58		
14	"	Speedy Transport Ltd	101113			1,729	60	257	60		
15	"	Johnsons' Plastic Products	101114			781	85	116	45		
16	"	Dawes Stationery	101115			120	97	18	02		
17	"	Office Supplies Ltd	101116			524	93	78	18		
18	"	Bank charges				259	64				
19	"	Bank interest				432	27				
20	"	Flood & Fire	S/O			1,255	77				
21	"	Plumy Motors Ltd	Banker's draft			72,450	27				
22	"	BACS salaries	BACS			55,327	92				

Solutions to practice devolved assessments

Purchases		Carriage		Bank charges interest		Telephone		Insurance		Motor expenses		Print, post & stationery		Wages and salaries		Fixed assets		Subsistence & sundry	
						43	20			233	47							60	80
						22	57			229	65							88	92
										205	15							113	17
										94	30							87	97
						28	72			131	92							10	00
		1,472	00																
665	40																		
												102	95						
												21	75			425	00		
				259	64														
				432	27														
								1,255	77										
										452	14					71,998	13		
														55,327	92				

200

SOLUTION TO PRACTICE DEVOLVED ASSESSMENT 3: CONWAY

Tutorial note. This devolved assessment tests your ability to write up a cash book. Do not forget the items on the bank statement that are not included on the list of payments!

Solution

(a) See Page 202.

(b) See Pages 203 to 204.

(c)

	£
Balance brought forward	28,742.45
Payments	(118,176.32)
Balance carried forward (overdraft)	(89,433.87)

System XX4 BANK PAYMENTS 31 July 20X5

N/C Name: BANK CURRENT ACCOUNT
1000

Tax rate: 17.5%
Batch Total: 118,176.32

N/C	DEP	DATE	CHEQUE	DETAILS	Net amount	Tax amount	Gross amount
4210		0407X5	113724	Armin Specialist	335.71	0.00	335.71
4170		0407X5	113725	Elwin Garden	4,425.78	0.00	4,425.78
4150		0407X5	113726	New Forest	12,840.33	0.00	12,840.33
4180		0507X5	113727	Leaver Garden	3,056.36	0.00	3,056.36
4160		0507X5	113728	Moss & Blythe	650.00	0.00	650.00
5560		1107X5	113729	M Payne	95.82	0.00	95.82
5560		1107X5	113730	W Bark	95.82	0.00	95.82
4140		1107X5	113731	Ric Aggregates	3,492.01	0.00	3,492.01
4200		1207X5	113732	Jackson & Brown	839.29	0.00	839.29
7220		1207X5	113733	Mack's Garage	21,567.45	0.00	21,567.45
4120		1207X5	113734	Chadwick Shrubs	87.13	0.00	87.13
4110		1207X5	113735	Water Garden	8,974.16	0.00	8,974.16
4160		1207X5	113736	Moss & Blythe	209.81	0.00	209.81
5520		1707X5	SO	Electricity Board	157.62	27.58	185.20
4180		1707X5	113737	Leaver Gardens	1,248.59	0.00	1,248.59
4190		1707X5	113738	Robinson Nurseries	5,697.05	0.00	5,697.05
4210		1707X5	113739	Armin Specialist	220.06	0.00	220.06
4220		1907X5	113740	Woodhouse	2,097.97	0.00	2,097.97
0000		1907X5	113741	CANCELLED	0.00	0.00	0.00
5550		1907X5	113742	British Telecom	102.53	17.94	120.47
4180		2507X5	113743	Leaver Garden	3,428.80	0.00	3,428.80
4160		2507X5	113744	Moss & Blythe	258.94	0.00	258.94
4140		2507X5	113745	RIC Aggregates	6,082.88	0.00	6,082.88
5510		2607X5	113746	British Gas	225.31	39.43	264.74
4120		2607X5	113747	Chadwick Shrubs	194.47	0.00	194.47
4130		3007X5	113748	Bishop's Plant Hire	8,309.90	0.00	8,309.90
5530		3007X5	DD	Rates	417.60	0.00	417.60
5570		3007X5	BACS	Salaries	31,721.82	0.00	31,721.82
6000		3007X5	113749	Petty Cash	327.66	0.00	327.66
5640		3107X5		Bank Charges	448.21	0.00	448.21
5540		3107X5	DD	Water	332.29	0.00	332.29
5640		3107X5		Overdraft fee	150.00	0.00	150.00
				TOTAL	118,091.37	84.95	118,176.32

Note: Remember purchase ledger items are analysed in the purchase ledger, not the cash book. This includes VAT.

The company can not reclaim VAT on a motor car.

JULY - PAYMENTS

	Date	Details	Cheque No	Total	VAT	Purchase Credit	Purchases Sundry
1	4 July	Armin Specialist Plants	113724	335.71		335.71	
2	"	Elwin Garden Supplies	113725	4,425.78		4,425.78	
3	"	New Forest Tree Nursery	113726	12,840.33		12,840.33	
4	5 July	Leaver Garden Tools	113727	3,056.36		3,056.36	
5	"	Moss & Blythe Nurseries	113728	650.00		650.00	
6	11 July	M Payne	113729	95.82		-	
7	"	W Bark	113730	95.82		-	
8	"	RIC Aggregates	113731	3,492.01		3,492.01	
9	12 July	Jackson & Brown Seeds	113732	839.29		839.29	
10	"	Mack's Garage	113733	21,567.45		-	
11	"	Chadwick Shrubs	113734	87.13		87.13	
12	"	Water Garden Specialists	113735	8,974.16		8,974.16	
13	"	Moss & Blythe Nurseries	113736	209.81		209.81	
14	17 July	Electricity Board	SO	185.20	27.58	-	
15	"	Leaver Garden Tools	113737	1,248.59		1,248.59	
16	"	Robinson Nurseries	113738	5,697.05		5,697.05	
17	"	Armin Specialist Plants	113739	220.06		220.06	
18	19 July	Woodhouse Building Supp.	113740	2,097.97		2,097.97	
19	"	CANCELLED	113741	-		-	
20	"	British Telecom	113742	120.47	17.94	-	
21	25 July	Leaver Garden Tools	113743	3,428.80		3,428.80	
22	"	Moss & Blythe Nurseries	113744	258.94		258.94	
23	"	RIC Aggregates	113745	6,082.88		6,082.88	
24	26 July	British Gas	113746	264.74	39.43	-	
25	"	Chadwick Shrubs	113747	194.47		194.47	
26	30 July	Bishops Plant Hire	113748	8,309.90		8,309.90	
27	"	Rates	DD	417.60			
28	"	Salaries	BACS	31,721.82			
29	"	Petty cash	113749	327.66			
30	31 July	Bank charges	-	598.21			
31	"	Water rates	DD	332.39			
32				118,176.32	84.95	62,449.24	
33							
34							

Solutions to practice devolved assessments

Heat & light	Bank charges interest	Telephone	Rates & water rates	Motor expenses	Print, post & stationery	Wages and salaries	Fixed Assets	Petty cash & Sundry
					95.82			
						95.82		
							21,567.45	
157.62								
		102.53						
225.31								
			417.60					
						31,721.82		
								327.66
	598.21							
			332.29					
382.93	598.21	102.53	749.89	-	-	31,913.46	21,567.45	327.66

4: Micawber

SOLUTION TO PRACTICE DEVOLVED ASSESSMENT 4: MICAWBER

Tutorial note. This Assessment addresses a number of aspects of accounting for goods and services received on credit. There is quite a lot of information which you must work through, but this should not present too much of a problem if you concentrate on what is required.

Solution

(a) (i) *Purchase ledger accounts*

SUPPLIER: COPPERFIELD				ACCOUNT NO: 87
Date	Batch/narrative	Trans Ref	£ (DR)/CR	£ Balance
1/6/X5	Balance b/f			991.99
3/6/X5	6/01	6032	792.11	1,784.10
5/6/X5	6/02	6055	175.60	1,959.70
9/6/X5	6/03	6178	264.47	2,224.17
11/6/X5	6/04	6216	737.02	2,961.19
11/6/X5	C6/1	100860	(834.91)	2,126.28

SUPPLIER: RUDGE				ACCOUNT NO: 121
Date	Batch/narrative	Trans Ref	£ (DR)/CR	£ Balance
1/6/X5	Balance b/f			876.40
11/6/X5	6/04	6215	1,152.83	2,029.23
11/6/X5	C6/1	100861	(366.66)	1,662.57

SUPPLIER: PIP				ACCOUNT NO: 104
Date	Batch/narrative	Trans Ref	£ (DR)/CR	£ Balance
1/6/X5	Balance b/f			655.30
9/6/X5	6/03	6190	843.00	1,498.30
11/6/X5	6/04	6214	257.87	1,756.17
11/6/X5	C6/1	100862	(545.30)	1,210.87

SUPPLIER: CRITCHLEY PLC				ACCOUNT NO: 42
Date	Batch/narrative	Trans Ref	£ (DR)/CR	£ Balance
1/6/X5	Balance b/f			15,071.93
11/6/X5	Man Chq 70912	JNL5	(8,000.00)	7,071.93
11/6/X5	Close down	JNL8	(7,071.93)	NIL

SUPPLIER: DORRIT				ACCOUNT NO: 89
Date	Batch/narrative	Trans Ref	£ (DR)/CR	£ Balance
1/6/X5	Balance b/f			4,509.90
3/6/X5	6/01	6001	410.11	4,920.01
5/6/X5	6/02	6053	973.75	5,893.76
11/6/95	6/04	6211	85.29	5,979.05
11/6/95	Contra	JNL8	(4,509.90)	1,469.15

Solutions to practice devolved assessments

SUPPLIER: NELL				ACCOUNT NO: 113
Date	Batch/narrative	Trans Ref	£ (DR)/CR	£ Balance
1/6/X5	Balance b/f			1,917.11
3/6/X5	6/01	6042	231.90	2,149.01
9/6/X5	6/03	6102	8.52	2,157.53
9/6/X5	R6/1	C/N 492	(20.20)	2,137.33
11/6/X5	6/04	6217	6,116.91	8,254.24
11/6/X5	C6/1	100863	(951.25)	7,302.99
11/6/X5	Pickwick	JNL8	(190.05)	7,112.94

SUPPLIER: SCROOGE				ACCOUNT NO: 131
Date	Batch/narrative	Trans Ref	£ (DR)/CR	£ Balance
1/6/X5	Balance b/f			7,759.50
11/6/X5	6/04	6210	72.90	7,832.40
11/6/X5	6/04	6213	11,422.61	19,255.01
11/6/X5	C6/1	100859	(5,312.20)	13,942.81

SUPPLIER: PICKWICK				ACCOUNT NO: 105
Date	Batch/narrative	Trans Ref	£ (DR)/CR	£ Balance
1/6/X5	Balance b/f			80.12
11/6/X5	6/04	6212	581.63	661.75
11/6/X5	R6/2	CN493	(500.00)	161.75
11/6/X5	Nell	JNL8	190.05	351.80

(ii) *Journals 11/6/X5*

Journals in respect of standard transactions

			Debit £	Credit £
1	Purchases		17,384.72	
	Creditors control			20,427.06
	VAT		3,042.34	

Being posting to N/L of PDB batch 6/04

			Debit £	Credit £
2	Purchases returns			425.53
	Creditors control		500.00	
	VAT			74.47

Being posting to N/L of PRDB batch R6/2

			Debit £	Credit £
3	Creditors control		8,010.32	
	Cash			8,010.32

Being posting to N/L of cheque list C6/1

			Debit £	Credit £
4	Creditors control		8,000.00	
	Cash			8,000.00

Being posting to N/L of manual cheques

			Debit £	Credit £
5	Critchley plc purchase ledger account		8,000.00	

Being memorandum account adjustment re JNL 4

Journals in respect of one-off adjustments

		Debit £	Credit £
6	Creditors control	7,071.93	
	Purchases (profit and loss account)		7,071.93

Being posting to N/L of debt write-off by supplier

		Debit £	Credit £
7	Purchase ledger control account	4,509.90	
	Sales ledger control account		4,509.90

Being contra between control accounts in N/L

		Debit £	Credit £
8	Critchley plc purchase ledger account	7,071.93	
	Dorrit purchase ledger account	4,509.90	
	Dorrit sales ledger account		4,509.90
	Nell purchase ledger account	190.05	
	Pickwick purchase ledger account		190.05

Being memorandum account adjustments re JNL 6 and JNL 7, together with correction of misposting of invoice (ref 4712)

(b) Micawber should take advantage of the discount:

(i) if doing so does not cause an overdraft; or

(ii) if the discount offered by Copperfield is greater than the overdraft charge and the company's relationship with the bank is such that the account can be used in this way.

	£	£
Bank balance	5,000	NIL
Less £10,000 × 99%	(9,900)	(9,900)
Bank overdraft	(4,900)	(9,900)
Bank charges per month, ie overdraft × 1.5%	(73.50)	(148.50)
Value of discount	100.00	100.00
Gain/(loss)	26.50	(48.50)

Therefore Micawber should take advantage of the discount if the current bank balance is £5,000, but not if the balance is nil.

5: Needham Baddely

SOLUTION TO PRACTICE DEVOLVED ASSESSMENT 5: NEEDHAM BADDELY

Tutorial note. There is a lot of information to digest in this assignment. It therefore demands a methodical approach, and you should be careful not to get side-tracked from the tasks set.

Solution

(a)

FROM:	NEEDHAM BADDELY LTD Skid Row Wantage, OX22 7PN	PURCHASE ORDER NO: 901
TO:	W E Gotham Components plc Old Iron Gate Street Wraillings Industrial Estate Melchett ATT: Sales Ledger	DATE: 3/9/X5
VAT REG:	6 721 3941	

Please supply the following.

Your product reference	Item	Quantity	Your list price £ p	Total (exc VAT) £ p
XLS 24	Grade 1 Widget 2 x 12	4	123.45	493.80
XLS 12	Grade 1 Widget 1 x 12	2	92.58	185.16
WMS 18	Magnetised sprocket	1	90.12	90.12
CER 870	Particle accelerator (CERN)	1	1,499.99	1,499.99
ENC 119	Neologism controller (ergonomic)	5	115.55	577.75
VET 999	Ultra-low energy Tardis motor	4	107.94	431.76
LEY 666	Low-energy Tardis motor	2-sp.off.	53.97	107.94 *
MYS E01	Single phase myco-simulator	9	675.05	6,075.45
PLX 200	Positive link extender 200	4-dis.	508.62	2,034.48 *

Total	11,496.45
Discounts and special offers *see workings attached*	*1,113.74
Net	10,382.71

Comments: *Particle Accelerator to First Court Street, Cambridge*
Remainder to Dairy Street, Milkington
Note: Special offers discounts for LEY 666 and PLX 200

Solutions to practice devolved assessments

Addendum to Order 901	
	£
Total list price	11,496.45
less Price of Low-energy Tardis Motors, which are free, with the special offer 1 for every 2 ultra-low energy Tardis Motors (2 × 53.97)	(107.94)
less 20% off the 4 Positive Link Extenders 200 (20% × £2,034.48)	(406.90)
	10,981.61
less 3% discount on first £2,000 =	(60.00)
less 6% discount on (£10,981.61 – £2,000)	(538.90)
	10,382.71
Total discounts and special offers are thus	107.94
	406.90
	60.00
	538.90
	1,113.74

(b) (i) Before VAT, you were estimating to pay £10,382.71.

However, the total, before VAT, of the two *invoices* you have received is:

	£
Invoice 7072	9,456.67
Invoice 7074	1,454.99
	10,911.66

You have therefore been invoiced for £528.95 (ignoring VAT) more than you had expected.

How do you find out what has gone wrong?

(1) Check the goods received notes to your order.

GRN no 9914 indicates that you have received *four* low-energy Tardis Motors as opposed to two. You have been billed for two, of course, and you have received two others on the special offer.

However, in your purchase orders and your workings, you indicated that *two* low-energy Tardis Motors were *all* that were required, and that you expected them to be supplied free of charge.

(2) W E Gotham plc has forgotten the 20% price reduction off the Positive Link Extenders.

(3) The discounts have been incorrectly calculated. The terms for the discounts are 3% off the first £2,000 and 6% off the rest of any *order*. Gotham have calculated the discount on an *invoice* basis.

We can now reconcile the discrepancies with the invoiced amounts and your order. Remember, the trade discounts must be calculated *after* the amounts for the special offers have been deducted.

Reconciliation

Total invoiced amount before VAT

	£
Invoice 7072	9,456.67
Invoice 7074	1,454.99
Total per W E Gotham plc invoices	10,911.66
Total per purchase order 901	10,382.71
Difference	528.95

5: Needham Baddely

Discounts and special offers

	£
Invoice 7072 (3% × £2,000) + 6% (£9,996.46 − £2,000)	539.79
Invoice 7074 3% × £1,499.99	45.00
Discounts and special offers per W E Gotham	584.79
Discounts and special offers per purchase order 901	1,113.74
Difference	528.95

The difference can be analysed as follows.

	£
Two extra low-energy Tardis Motors	107.94
20% discount on Positive Link Extenders (per part (a))	406.90
	514.84
Less 6% discount given on £514.84	(30.89)
Invoice 7074 *additional* discount on £1,499.99 of 3% (to make it up to 6%)	45.00
	528.95

(ii) You could take the following action.

(1) Phone W E Gotham plc with your queries.

(2) Ask them for a credit note.

(3) If necessary send them supporting documentation (eg your calculations).

(4) Ask them to take back the extra low-energy Tardis Motors, if you have no further use for them, as they might be using up expensive storage space, and you do not want to be deemed to have accepted them.

Solutions to practice devolved assessments

(c)

NEEDHAM BADDELY

GOODS RECEIVED NOTE

Site: Glastonbury   No: ①

Date: October 20X5 ②

Item	Code	Quantity	Purchase Order No
Circuit extender link 25	③ CXL25	4	931
Particle accelerator - TORUS	6911 ④	1	940
7-phase myco-simulator	7519	⑤	920
Rhombord oscillating widget	5655	1	896
Anoid oscillating widget	⑥ 6565	7	896
Phenomenology inhibitor	1001	3	896
Magnetised sprocket	3842	1	941
Circuit training pump	9810 ⑦	9	637
Particle accelerator - CERN	5911 ⑧	4	⑨
Sonic orgone negater	0825	6	639

(1) No GRN number.

(2) Date incomplete.

(3) Not a stock code used in Needham Baddely's systems. In fact, it is the stock code used by W E Gotham.

(4) The code of a Torus-compatible particle accelerator is 5911, not 6911.

(5) No quantity - even if only one has been received, it is best to say so.

(6) Coding error. It should be 6655 not 6565.

(7) Coding error. The correct code is 8910.

(8) A CERN-compatible particle accelerator has the code 4911.

(9) No purchase order reference. Although items may be listed on a single purchase order, this does not mean that they will be delivered at the same time.

(d) (i)

	£
Balance per Ergonome Ltd at 1 October 20X5	5,227.10
Invoice 8743 not posted to purchase ledger, because the invoice is Addressed to D E Fences Ltd not Needham Baddely Ltd (100kg on 24 July 20X5, GRN G1724)	(2,350.00)
Duplicate invoice 8379, supported by Goods Received Note G1672 appears not to have been posted to Needham Baddely Ltd's Purchase ledger (not received when purchase ledger extract taken)	(1,060.71)
Debit note 901 for faulty goods, not processed by Ergonome Ltd	(1,562.49)
Balance per Needham Baddely at 30 September 20X5	253.90

(ii) Now that the two balances have been reconciled, corrections have to be made, which both parties must agree to.

Needham Baddely has omitted to post an invoice for £1,060.71. This should be rectified immediately. Ergonome Ltd must amend their records to cancel invoice 8743 and to recognise the debit note raised. At the same time, as these were faulty goods, Ergonome Ltd should take the goods back.

Consequently, a letter ought to be written to Ergonome Ltd to sort out the situation. As the finance director of Ergonome Ltd has written in person, somebody equally senior in Needham Baddely should sign the letter.

(iii)

>
> **Needham Baddely Ltd**
> **Skid Row**
> **Wantage**
> **OX22 7PN**
>
> 3 October 20X5
>
> I Faraday Esq
> Finance Director
> Ergonome Ltd
> Fonda House
> 12 Angrimen Street
> Pleading
> Lincs
>
> Dear Mr Faraday
>
> Thank you for your letter of 2 October 29X5. May I assure you that recourse to solicitors is not necessary for our account with you to be sorted out.
>
> We have examined in detail your statement as at 30 September 20X5 and have compared it to our records.
>
> You have double invoiced us an amount of £2,350.00 (your invoice number 8743). This relates to a delivery of Kryptonite Nuggets already billed on invoice 8742. Also, you have not recorded our debit note (our ref 901 dated 3 August 20X5) of £1,562.49 which we have sent to you to cover the value of faulty goods received. A cheque for £1,375.01 has been received by yourselves for the remainder.
>
> On our side, we have omitted to post invoice number 8379, of which a duplicate was sent to us. It arrived by separate post, the day before your letter. It has been agreed to the relevant GRN and we will enter it to our records forthwith.
>
> To conclude, our balance with you at 30 September 20X5 is rightly stated as follows.
>
> | | £ |
> |---|---|
> | Invoice 8379 | 1,060.71 |
> | Invoice 8912 | 253.90 |
> | | 1,314.61 |
>
> You might be interested to know that a cheque to cover invoice 8912 has been posted recently.
>
> If you have any further queries please do not hesitate to get in touch.
>
> Yours sincerely
>
> *L Legg*
>
> Lucas Legg
> Chief Accountant

Note: Remember to be polite. Even if the letter from Ergonome Ltd was threatening, there is no need to respond in kind. There are faults on both sides and a letter setting out the problems (and showing that you have paid what you consider to be due), will be far more effective.

Solutions to trial run devolved assessments

SOLUTIONS TO TRIAL RUN DEVOLVED ASSESSMENT 1

BARKERS

DO NOT TURN THIS PAGE UNTIL YOU HAVE COMPLETED THE TRIAL RUN DEVOLVED ASSESSMENT

SOLUTIONS

Task 1: Remittance advices

14723

REMITTANCE ADVICE

Barkers Limited
Dalmation Road
Wagford
01729 35160

TO: Fifi's Fluffy Fillings
Foam Road
Softall

Account No: B72 Date: 30.4.X5 Page: 1

DATE	DETAILS		INVOICES £	CREDIT NOTES £	PAYMENT AMOUNT £
3.4.X5	Invoice	7142	102.95		102.95
16.4.X5	Invoice	7210	35.63		35.63
23.4.X5	Invoice	7242	197.52		197.52
	TOTAL		336.10		336.10

14724

REMITTANCE ADVICE

Barkers Limited
Dalmation Road
Wagford
01729 35160

TO: Tree Top Timber Ltd
Yew Street
Ashford

Account No: T713 Date: 30.4.X5 Page: 1

DATE	DETAILS		INVOICES	CREDIT NOTES	PAYMENT AMOUNT
3.4.X5	Invoice	97820	40.50		40.50
11.4.X5	Invoice	97857	155.60		155.60
21.4.X5	invoice	97892	350.44		350.44
22.4.X5	Invoice	97911	14.52		14.52
25.4.X5	Invoice	97925	180.14		180.14
26.4.X5	Credit Note	CN7751		121.60	-121.60
27.4.X5	Invoice	98011	215.10		215.10
	Discount @ 5%			13.68	-13.68
	Discount @ 2%			7.30	-7.30
			956.30	142.58	813.72

Discount @ 5% = £(180.14 + 215.10 - 121.60) x 5% = £13.68
Discount @ 2% = £(14.52 + 350.44) x 2% = £7.30

14725

REMITTANCE ADVICE

Barkers Limited
Dalmation Road
Wagford
01729 35160

TO: Nick's Nails
Hammer Road
Bangington

Account No: B11510 Date: 30.4.X5 Page: 1

DATE	DETAILS		INVOICES £	CREDIT NOTES £	PAYMENT AMOUNT £
1.4.X5	Invoice	N7252	40.22		40.22
7.4.X5	Invoice	N7263	21.50		21.50
19.4.X5	Invoice	N7292	14.90		14.90
21.4.X5	Credit note	CN7210		11.50	-11.50
28.4.X5	Invoice	N7321	11.50		11.50
	Discount @ 8.5%			1.27	-1.27
	TOTAL		88.12	12.77	75.35

Discount @ 8.5% = £(14.90 + 11.50 - 11.50) x 8.5% = £1.27

1: Barkers (solutions)

Tasks 2 and 3: **Payment authorisation stamps**

(i) FIFI'S FLUFFY FILLINGS

```
        INVOICE PAYMENT
          APPROVED BY
Name     Mrs Growler
Comments Pay all invoices
Date     30.4.X5
                        Initials  BG
```

(ii) TREE TOP TIMBER LIMITED

```
        INVOICE PAYMENT
          APPROVED BY
Name     Bulldog Barker
Comments Do not pay January and March
Date     30.4.X5           Invoices
                        Initials  BB
```

(iii) NICK'S NAILS

```
        INVOICE PAYMENT
          APPROVED BY
Name     Mrs B Growler
Comments Pay all invoices
Date     30.4.X5
                        Initials  BG
```

The following supporting documentation is required.
(i) VAT invoices for petrol and dinner
(ii) Receipts for parking and taxis

Mr Marrow, the sales director, should authorise the claim.

Task 4: **Cheque requisition form**

```
                                                  247324
                 Cheque Requisition

        Date      20 April 20X5
        Payable to  Win. A. Lot
        Amount     £157.02
        Details    Expenses for April


        Signed     Any of the directors, but preferably Mr Marrow
```

Solutions to trial run devolved assessements

Task 5: Payment authorisation stamp

```
INVOICE PAYMENT
   APPROVED BY
Name     T Bone
Comments Pay
Date     30.4.X5
                    Initials   TB
```

Task 6: Bank giro credit payment slip

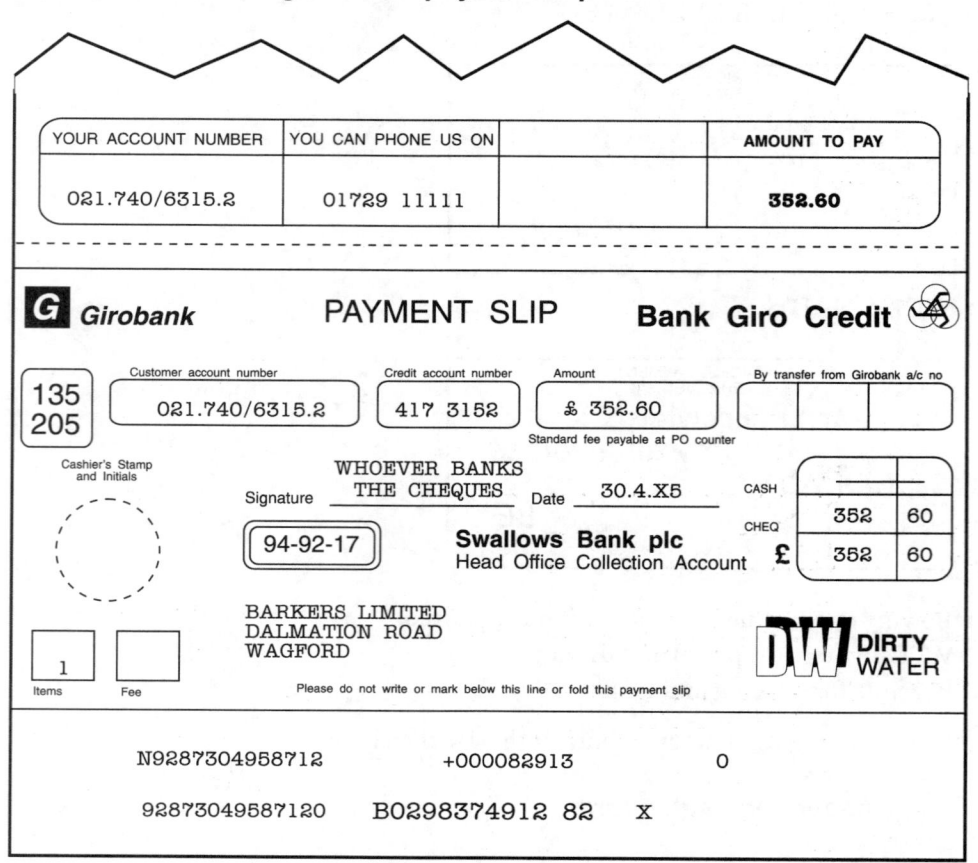

YOUR ACCOUNT NUMBER	YOU CAN PHONE US ON		AMOUNT TO PAY
021.740/6315.2	01729 11111		352.60

G Girobank — PAYMENT SLIP — Bank Giro Credit

135 / 205

- Customer account number: 021.740/6315.2
- Credit account number: 417 3152
- Amount: £ 352.60
- Standard fee payable at PO counter
- By transfer from Girobank a/c no: [ ]

Signature: WHOEVER BANKS THE CHEQUES
Date: 30.4.X5
94-92-17

Swallows Bank plc
Head Office Collection Account

CASH / CHEQ: 352.60 / £ 352.60

BARKERS LIMITED
DALMATION ROAD
WAGFORD

DW DIRTY WATER

Items: 1   Fee:

Please do not write or mark below this line or fold this payment slip

N9287304958712   +000082913   0
92873049587120   B0298374912 82   X

Task 7: Cheques

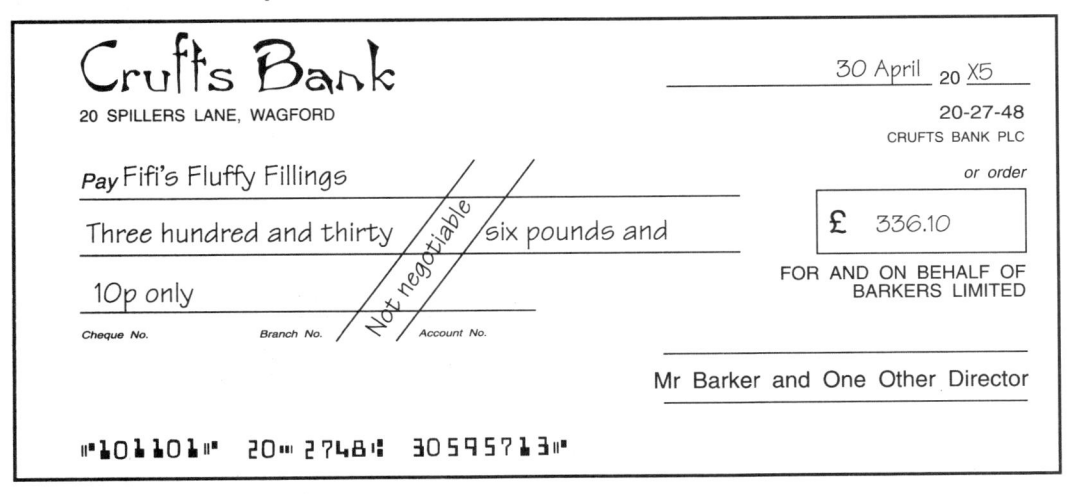

Crufts Bank
20 SPILLERS LANE, WAGFORD

30 April 20 X5
20-27-48
CRUFTS BANK PLC

Pay Fifi's Fluffy Fillings   or order

Three hundred and thirty six pounds and 10p only

£ 336.10

FOR AND ON BEHALF OF BARKERS LIMITED

Not negotiable

Cheque No.   Branch No.   Account No.

Mr Barker and One Other Director

⑈101101⑈ 20⑆2748⑊ 30595713⑈

Crufts Bank
20 SPILLERS LANE, WAGFORD

30 April 20 X5
20-27-48
CRUFTS BANK PLC

Pay Tree Top Timber Limited   or order

Eight hundred and thirteen pounds and 72 pence only

£ 813.72

FOR AND ON BEHALF OF BARKERS LIMITED

Not negotiable

Cheque No.   Branch No.   Account No.

Mr Barker and one other Director

⑈101102⑈ 20⑆2748⑊ 30595713⑈

Crufts Bank
20 SPILLERS LANE, WAGFORD

30 April 20 X5
20-27-48
CRUFTS BANK PLC

Pay Nick's Nails   or order

Seventy five pounds and 35p only

£ 75.35

FOR AND ON BEHALF OF BARKERS LIMITED

Not negotiable

Cheque No.   Branch No.   Account No.

Any two Directors

⑈101103⑈ 20⑆2748⑊ 30595713⑈

Solutions to trial run devolved assessements

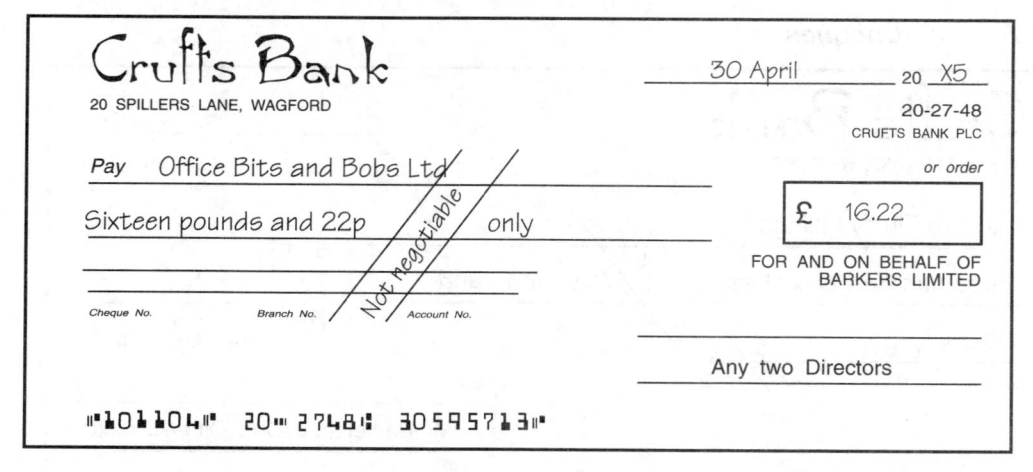

Cheque 1

Crufts Bank
20 SPILLERS LANE, WAGFORD
30 April 20 X5
20-27-48
CRUFTS BANK PLC

Pay Office Bits and Bobs Ltd   or order
Sixteen pounds and 22p only
£ 16.22

Not negotiable

FOR AND ON BEHALF OF BARKERS LIMITED

Any two Directors

101104 20-2748 30595713

Cheque 2

Crufts Bank
20 SPILLERS LANE, WAGFORD
30 April 20 X5
20-27-48
CRUFTS BANK PLC

Pay Dirty Water   or order
Three hundred and fifty two pounds and 60p
£ 352.60

Not negotiable

FOR AND ON BEHALF OF BARKERS LIMITED

Mr Barker and one other Director

101105 20-2748 30595713

Cheque 3

Crufts Bank
20 SPILLERS LANE, WAGFORD
30 April 20 X5
20-27-48
CRUFTS BANK PLC

Pay Win A Lot   or order
One hundred and fifty seven pounds and 2p only
£ 157.02

FOR AND ON BEHALF OF BARKERS LIMITED

Any two Directors

101106 20-2748 30595713

1: Barkers (solutions)

Tasks 8, 10 and 11

Manual cash book: payments

APRIL - PAYMENTS

	Date	Details	Cheque number	Discounts Received	Total	VAT	Creditors	Petty cash	Bank Charges Interest	Telephone	Rent, rates and water rates	Motor expenses	Print, post & stationary	Wages and salaries	Subsistence and sundry
1	30.4	Petty Cash	101100		84 23			84 23							
2	30.4	Fifi's Fluffy Fillings	101101		336 10		336 10								
3	30.4	Tree Top Timber Limited	101102	20 98	813 72		813 72								
4	30.4	Nick's Nails	101103	1 27	75 35		75 35								
5	30.4	Office Bits & Bobs	101104		16 22	2 42							13 80		
6	30.4	Dirty Water	101105		352 60						352 60				
7	30.4	Win A Lot	101106		157 02	19 52						70 50			67 00
8															
9	18.4	British Telecom	DD		120 00	17 87				102 13					
10	30.4	Doberman Mat Company	SO		100 00	14 89					85 11				
11	30.4	Rates	DD		50 00						50 00				
12	30.4	BACS Salaries			1251 00									1251 00	
13															
14															
15															
16															
17															
18															
19															
20															
21															
22				22 25	3356 24	54 70	1,225 17	84 23		102 13	487 71	70 50	13 80	1251 00	67 00

Solutions to trial run devolved assessments

Task 9: Petty cash vouchers

Voucher No 153
Petty Cash Voucher
Date: 3/4/X5
- Cleaner — £5.00
Total: £5.00
Signature: B Growler
Authorised by: R Cash

Voucher No 154
Petty Cash Voucher
Date: 3/4/X5
- Impress Dairy (Milk) — £3.90
Total: £3.90
Signature: P Pant
Authorised by: R Cash

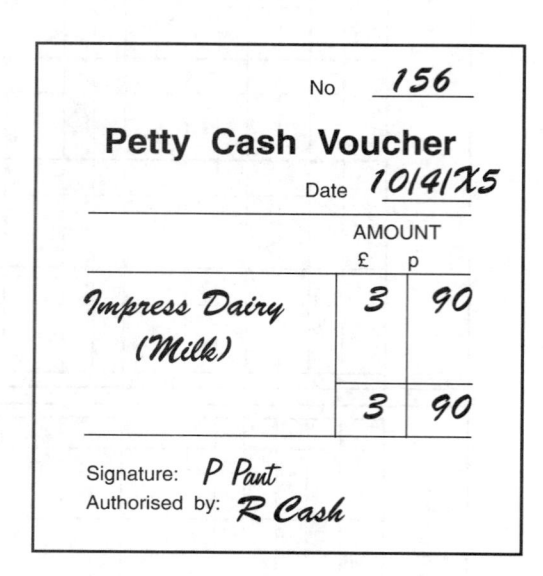

Voucher No 155
Petty Cash Voucher
Date: 10/4/X5
- Cleaner — £5.00
Total: £5.00
Signature: P Pant
Authorised by: R Cash

Voucher No 156
Petty Cash Voucher
Date: 10/4/X5
- Impress Dairy (Milk) — £3.90
Total: £3.90
Signature: P Pant
Authorised by: R Cash

Voucher No 157
Petty Cash Voucher
Date: 15/4/X5
- Coffee, tea etc — £12.05
Total: £12.05
Signature: P Pant
Authorised by: R Cash

Voucher No 158
Petty Cash Voucher
Date: 17/4/X5
- Cleaner — £5.00
Total: £5.00
Signature: P Pant
Authorised by: R Cash

1: Barkers (solutions)

Petty Cash Voucher No 159
Date 17/4/X5

	AMOUNT £	p
Impress Dairy (Milk)	3	90
	3	90

Signature: P Pant
Authorised by: R Cash

Petty Cash Voucher No 160
Date 22/4/X5

	AMOUNT £	p
Rusty's Hardware (cleaning materials)	26	06
VAT	4	56
	30	62

Signature: P Pant
Authorised by: T Bone

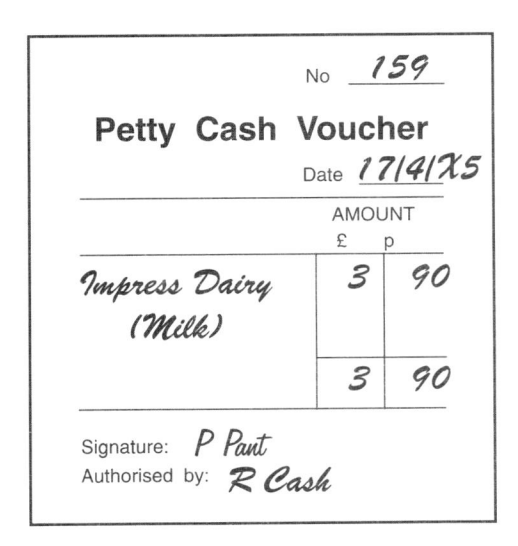

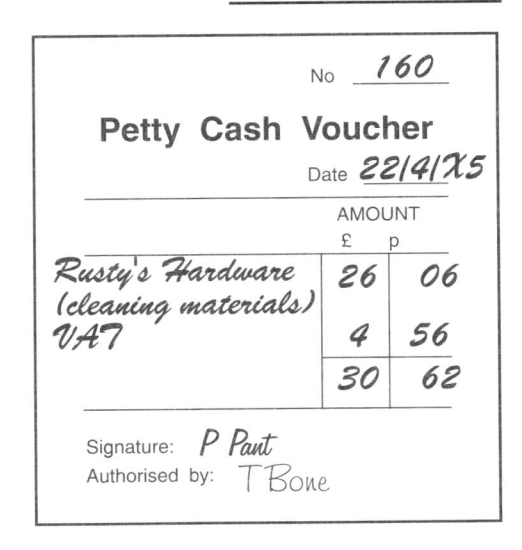

Petty Cash Voucher No 161
Date 22/4/X5

	AMOUNT £	p
Post Office (stamps)	5	96
	5	96

Signature: B Growler
Authorised by: R Cash

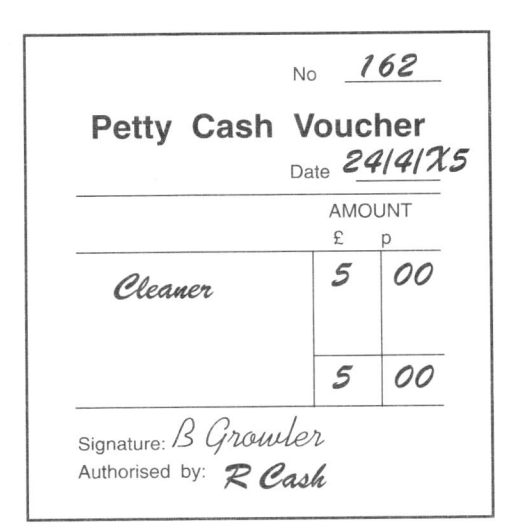

Petty Cash Voucher No 162
Date 24/4/X5

	AMOUNT £	p
Cleaner	5	00
	5	00

Signature: B Growler
Authorised by: R Cash

Petty Cash Voucher No 163
Date 24/4/X5

	AMOUNT £	p
Impress Dairy (Milk)	3	90
	3	90

Signature: P Pant
Authorised by: R Cash

Tutorial note. It would not be appropriate to pay the bill from the Pedigree Wine Bar through Petty Cash since it is over the £50 limit. Win A Lot should obtain reimbursement through an expense claim.

Solutions to trial run devolved assessements

Task 9: Petty cash book page

PETTY CASH BOOK

Details	Net receipt £	VAT £	Total £	Date	Details	Voucher No	Total £	VAT £	Analysis of payments			
									Wages & salaries £	Subsistence and sundry £	Print, post and stationery £
Balance b/f			100.00	3.4	Cleaner	153	5.00		5.00		
				3.4	Impress dairy	154	3.90			3.90	
				10.4	Cleaner	155	5.00		5.00		
				10.4	Impress dairy	156	3.90			3.90	
				15.4	Coffee, tea etc	157	12.05			12.05	
				17.4	Cleaner	158	5.00		5.00		
				17.4	Impress dairy	159	3.90			3.90	
				22.4	Rusty's Hardware	160	30.62	4.56		26.06	
				22.4	Post office (stamps)	161	5.96				5.96
				24.4	Cleaner	162	5.00		5.00		
				24.4	Impress dairy	163	3.90			3.90	
			84.23				84.23	4.56	20.00	53.71	5.96
Cash			184.23	30.4	Balance c/d		100.00				
							184.23				

1: Barkers (solutions)

Tasks 9 and 11
Main ledger accounts

Creditors control account

Date	Details	Amount £	Date	Details	Amount £
30 April 20X5	Purchase returns day book	133.10	1 April 20X5	Balance b/f	226.01
30 April 20X5	Cash book	1,225.17	30 April 20X5	Purchase day book	1,380.52
30 April 20X5	Discounts received	22.25			
30 April 20X5	Balance c/f	226.01			
		1,606.53			1,606.53
			1 May 20X5	Balance b/f	226.01

Print, post and stationery

Date	Details	Amount £	Date	Details	Amount £
1 April 20X5	Balance b/f	40.56			
30 April 20X5	Cash book	13.80			
30 April 20X5	Petty cash book	5.96	30 April 20X5	Balance c/f	60.32
		60.32			60.32
1 May 20X5	Balance b/f	60.32			

Rent, rates and water rates

Date	Details	Amount £	Date	Details	Amount £
1 April 20X5	Balance b/f	654.37			
30 April 20X5	Cash book	487.71	30 April 20X5	Balance c/f	1,142.08
		1,142.08			1,142.08
1 May 20X5	Balance b/f	1,142.08			

Solutions to trial run devolved assessements

Telephone

Date	Details	Amount £	Date	Details	Amount £
1 April 20X5	Balance b/f	452.84			
30 April 20X5	Cash book	102.13	30 April 20X5	Balance c/f	554.97
		554.97			554.97
1 May 20X5	Balance b/f	554.97			

Motor expenses

Date	Details	Amount £	Date	Details	Amount £
1 April 20X5	Balance b/f	212.80			
30 April 20X5	Cash book	70.50	30 April 20X5	Balance c/f	283.30
		283.30			283.30
1 May 20X5	Balance b/f	283.30			

Wages and salaries

Date	Details	Amount £	Date	Details	Amount £
1 April 20X5	Balance b/f	6,850.25			
30 April 20X5	Cash book	1,251.00			
30 April 20X5	Petty cash book	20.00	30 April 20X5	Balance c/f	8,121.25
		8,121.25			8,121.25
1 May 20X5	Balance b/f	8,121.25			

Subsistence and sundry

Date	Details	Amount £	Date	Details	Amount £
1 April 20X5	Balance b/f	473.48			
30 April 20X5	Cash book	67.00			
30 April 20X5	Petty cash book	53.71	30 April 20X5	Balance c/f	594.19
		594.19			594.19
1 May 20X5	Balance b/f	594.19			

VAT

Date	Details	Amount £	Date	Details	Amount £
30 April 20X5	Purchase day book	181.43	1 April 20X5	Balance b/f	586.48
30 April 20X5	Cash book	54.70	30 April 20X5	Sales day book	352.51
30 April 20X5	Petty cash book	4.56	30 April 20X5	Cash book receipts	200.51
30 April 20X5	Balance c/f	898.81			
		1,139.50			1,139.50
			1 May 20X5	Balance b/f	898.81

Discounts received

Date	Details	Amount £	Date	Details	Amount £
			1 April 20X5	Balance b/f	121.07
30 April 20X5	Balance c/f	143.32	30 April 20X5	Creditors control a/c	22.25
		143.32			143.32
			1 May 20X5	Balance b/f	143.32

Solutions to trial run devolved assessments

ASSESSMENT CRITERIA

Task 1

Remittance advices must be correctly prepared. No more than three errors in total.

Task 2

Authorisation obtained.

Tasks 3 and 4

Correct documentation and authorisation must be obtained. Cheque requisition should be accurately prepared. Only one error allowed.

Task 5

Approval obtained.

Task 6

The bank giro credit should be accurately prepared. Only one error is allowed.

Task 7

Cheques should be accurately prepared. Only two errors allowed in total.

Task 8

Cash payments must be correctly entered and totalled. Only two calculation errors allowed.

Task 9

Vouchers correctly prepared and details entered into the cash book (two errors allowed). Cash book correctly totalled and balanced off (two calculation errors allowed). Totals transferred to the main ledger accounts (one error allowed).

Task 10

Correct postings should be made. One error or omission allowed.

Task 11

Cash books balanced off and totals posted to the main ledger accounts. Only one error allowed.

SOLUTIONS TO TRIAL RUN DEVOLVED ASSESSMENT 2

BEST-BOOKS

DO NOT TURN THIS PAGE UNTIL YOU HAVE COMPLETED THE TRIAL RUN DEVOLVED ASSESSMENT

SOLUTIONS

TASK 1

Suppliers invoices to check	Action
Pronto Press Ltd	Invoice can be passed to J Ross for authorisation.
Super Stationery Supplies Ltd	VAT has been calculated on the gross figure not the discounted figure. VAT should be £21.54 not £23.93. Return invoice to supplier.
Beautiful Books plc	*Accounting for beginners* should read £593.25 not £586.25 and the total invoice value is £843.85 not £836.85. Return invoice to supplier.

TASK 2

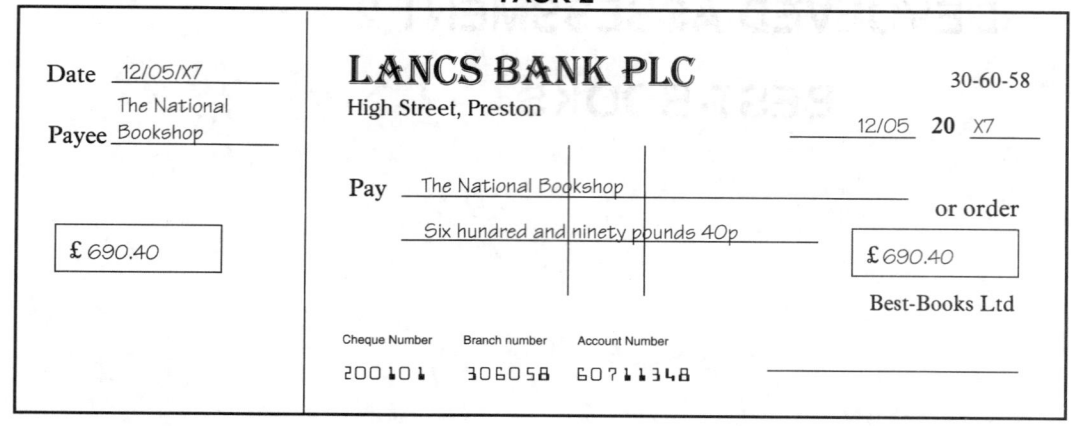

Date: 12/05/X7
Payee: The National Bookshop
£690.40

LANCS BANK PLC
High Street, Preston
30-60-58
12/05 20 X7

Pay: The National Bookshop
Six hundred and ninety pounds 40p
or order
£690.40
Best-Books Ltd

Cheque Number: 200101
Branch number: 306058
Account Number: 60711348

2: Best-Books (solutions)

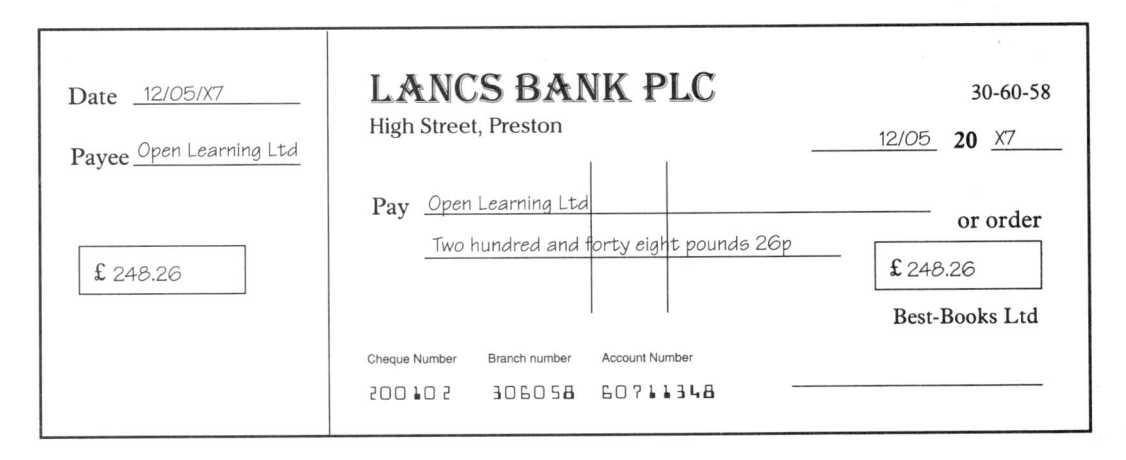

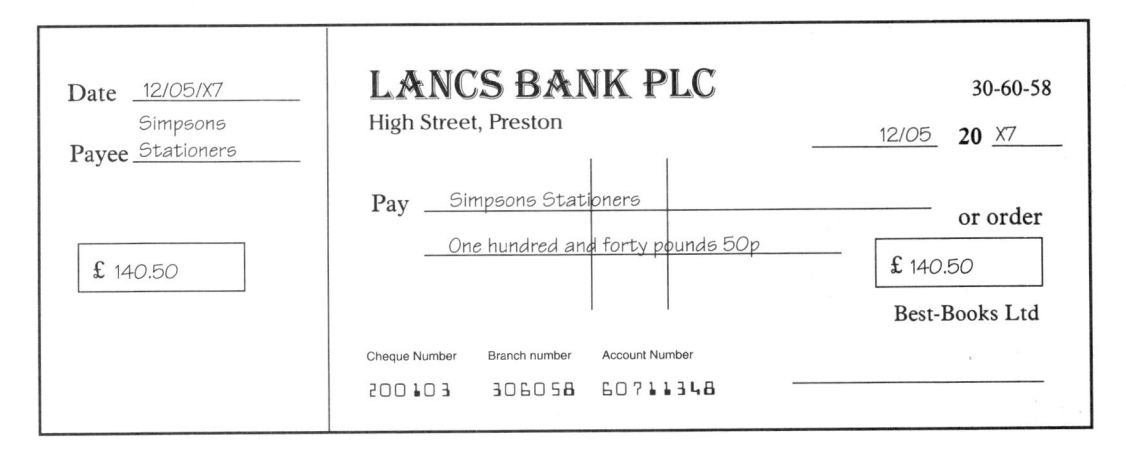

Cheque 1:
- Date: 12/05/X7
- Payee: Open Learning Ltd
- Amount: £248.26
- LANCS BANK PLC, High Street, Preston — 30-60-58
- Date: 12/05 20 X7
- Pay: Open Learning Ltd
- Two hundred and forty eight pounds 26p
- £248.26
- Best-Books Ltd
- Cheque Number: 200102
- Branch number: 306058
- Account Number: 60711348

Cheque 2:
- Date: 12/05/X7
- Payee: Simpsons Stationers
- Amount: £140.50
- LANCS BANK PLC, High Street, Preston — 30-60-58
- Date: 12/05 20 X7
- Pay: Simpsons Stationers
- One hundred and forty pounds 50p
- £140.50
- Best-Books Ltd
- Cheque Number: 200103
- Branch number: 306058
- Account Number: 60711348

TASK 3

Creditors ledger

PRONTO PRESS LTD

		£			£
14 April	Bank	105.40	1 April	Bal b/d	294.51
19 April	Bank	110.62	8 April	Purchases	206.48
26 April	Bank	1,848.08	14 April	Purchases	1,539.42
30 April	Bal c/d	171.00	20 April	Purchases	194.69
		2,235.10			2,235.10
			1 May	Bal b/d	171.00

TASK 4

Pronto Press Ltd

	£
Balance as per creditors ledger	171.00
Add: Payment to Pronto Press not yet recorded	1,848.08
	2,019.08
Less: Purchases not yet recorded by Pronto Press	(194.69)
Balance as per statement of account	1,824.39

Solutions to trial run devolved assessments

TASK 5

Petty cash book

Receipts		Date	Details	Amount
£				£
Bal b/d	150.00	April		
		1	Telephone	2.40
		7	Postage	8.29
		8	Travel	11.40
		10	Postage	9.30
		12	Newspapers	1.49
		17	Tea/coffee	6.45
		20	Milk	2.19
		24	Postage	8.90
		24	Travel	4.25
		24	Postage	11.98
		27	Milk	2.19
				68.84
Bal b/d	81.16			
Bank	68.84			
Bal c/d	150.00			

TASK 6

Two column cash book

Date	Details	Cash	Bank	Date	Details	Cash	Bank
		£	£			£	£
01/04/X7	Bal b/d	21.90		01/04/X7	Bal b/d		101.45
08/04/X7	Contra		200.00	02/04/X7	Stationery	11.50	
19/04/X7	Contra		300.00	05/04/X7	Creditors		891.56
28/04/X7	Contra		100.00	08/04/X7	Contra	200.00	
28/04/X7	Misc. receipts	659.26	2,217.44	11/04/X7	Creditors		196.51
				15/04/X7	Salaries		296.50
				16/04/X7	Inland Revenue		290.61
				19/04/X7	Contra	300.00	
				24/04/X7	Creditors		490.65
				28/04/X7	Contra	100.00	
				30/04/X7	Bal c/d	69.66	550.16
		681.16	2,817.44			681.16	2,817.44
01/05/X7	Bal b/d	69.66	550.16				

ASSESSMENT CRITERIA

Task 1

The two suppliers' invoices which include errors must be identified.

Task 2

The three cheques must be completed accurately and neatly with no more than one error allowed.

Task 3

The ledgers must be completed accurately and balances carried down to the next period of account.

Task 4

Only a correct reconciliation is enough to demonstrate competence.

Task 5

All the details must be entered correctly into the petty cash book and the Imprest account balanced to £150.

Task 6

The two column cash book must be filled in neatly and accurately. Not more than one error permitted.

Overall assessment

You may be allowed to make further minor errors, provided you do not suggest a fundamental lack of understanding.

You will not be penalised more than once for the same error. If you transfer an incorrect figure to another part of the exercise, this is not counted as a further error.

SOLUTIONS TO TRIAL RUN DEVOLVED ASSESSMENT 3

GROW-EASY

DO NOT TURN THIS PAGE UNTIL YOU HAVE COMPLETED THE TRIAL RUN DEVOLVED ASSESSMENT

SOLUTIONS

TASK 1

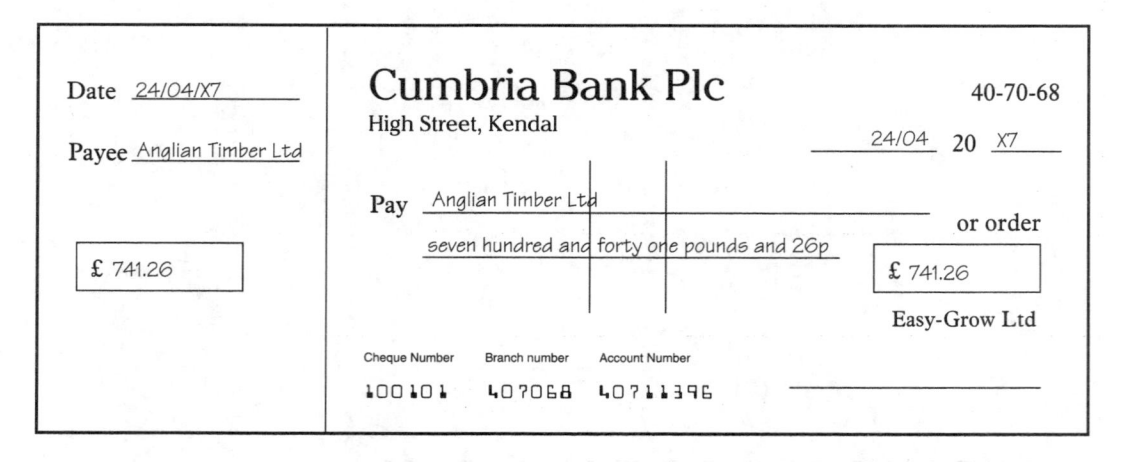

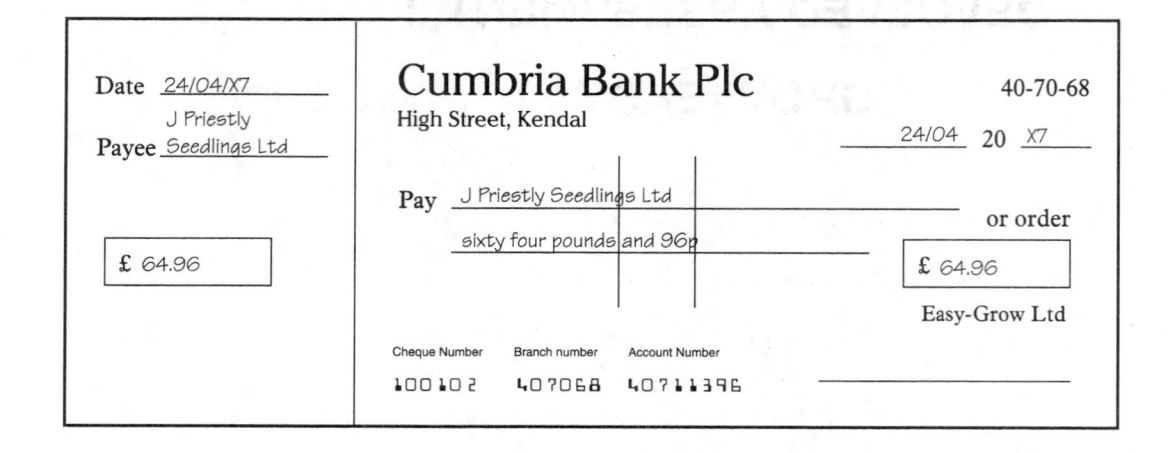

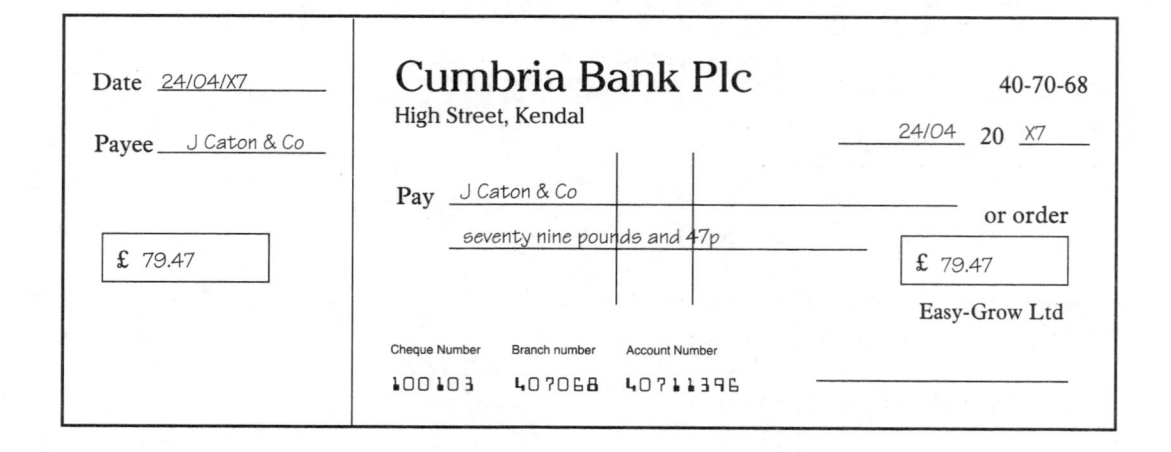

Cheque 1 (counterfoil and cheque)

Counterfoil:
- Date: 24/04/X7
- Payee: Anglian Timber Ltd
- £ 741.26

Cheque:
- Cumbria Bank Plc, High Street, Kendal
- 40-70-68
- Date: 24/04 20 X7
- Pay: Anglian Timber Ltd — or order
- seven hundred and forty one pounds and 26p
- £ 741.26
- Easy-Grow Ltd
- Cheque Number: 100101
- Branch number: 407068
- Account Number: 40711396

Cheque 2 (counterfoil and cheque)

Counterfoil:
- Date: 24/04/X7
- Payee: J Priestly Seedlings Ltd
- £ 64.96

Cheque:
- Cumbria Bank Plc, High Street, Kendal
- 40-70-68
- Date: 24/04 20 X7
- Pay: J Priestly Seedlings Ltd — or order
- sixty four pounds and 96p
- £ 64.96
- Easy-Grow Ltd
- Cheque Number: 100102
- Branch number: 407068
- Account Number: 40711396

Cheque 3 (counterfoil and cheque)

Counterfoil:
- Date: 24/04/X7
- Payee: J Caton & Co
- £ 79.47

Cheque:
- Cumbria Bank Plc, High Street, Kendal
- 40-70-68
- Date: 24/04 20 X7
- Pay: J Caton & Co — or order
- seventy nine pounds and 47p
- £ 79.47
- Easy-Grow Ltd
- Cheque Number: 100103
- Branch number: 407068
- Account Number: 40711396

3: Grow-Easy (solutions)

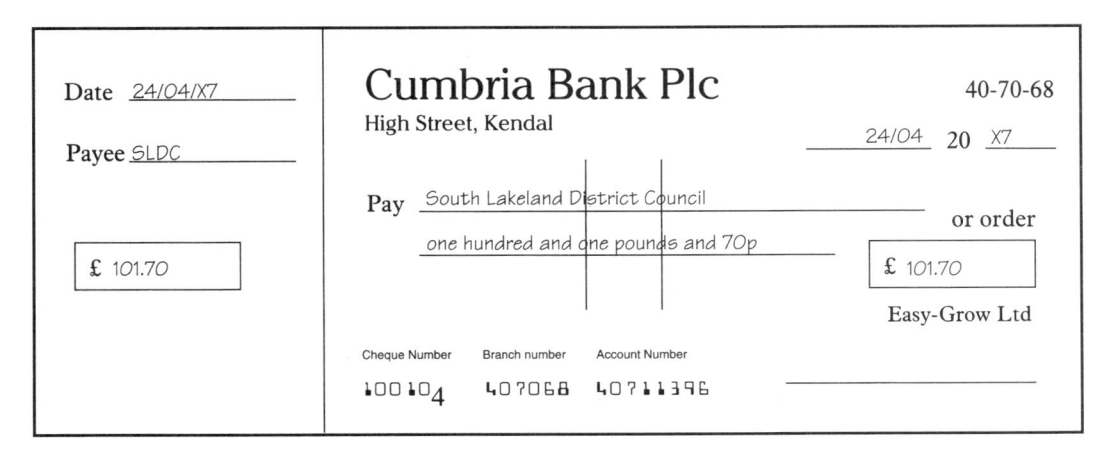

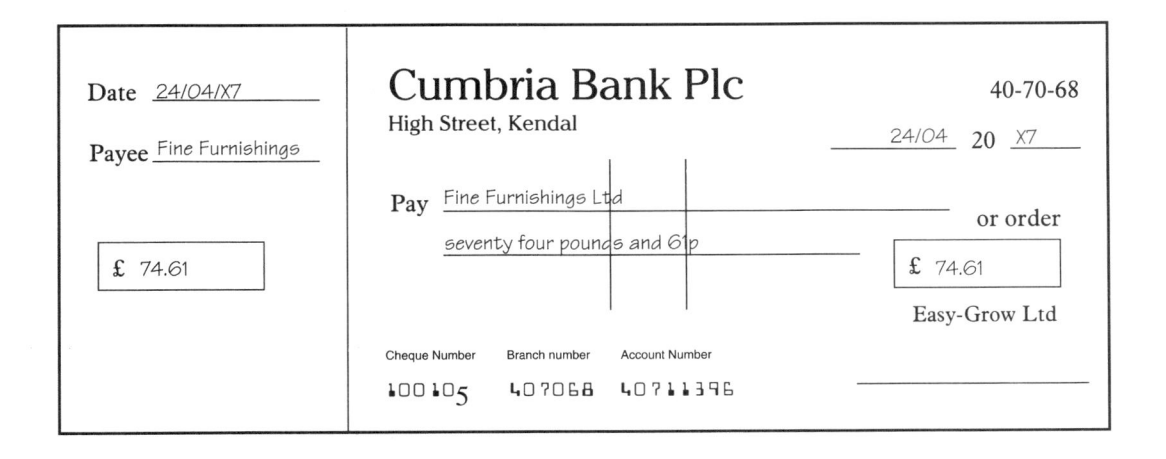

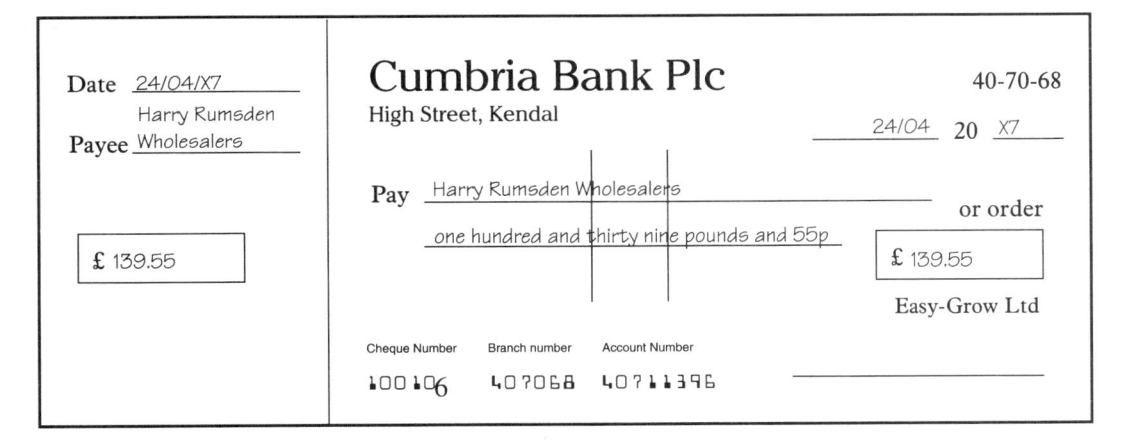

Cheque 100104
Date: 24/04/X7
Payee: SLDC
£ 101.70

Cumbria Bank Plc — 40-70-68
High Street, Kendal
24/04 20 X7
Pay South Lakeland District Council or order
one hundred and one pounds and 70p
£ 101.70
Easy-Grow Ltd
Cheque Number 100104 Branch number 40 7068 Account Number 40711396

Cheque 100105
Date: 24/04/X7
Payee: Fine Furnishings
£ 74.61

Cumbria Bank Plc — 40-70-68
High Street, Kendal
24/04 20 X7
Pay Fine Furnishings Ltd or order
seventy four pounds and 61p
£ 74.61
Easy-Grow Ltd
Cheque Number 100105 Branch number 40 7068 Account Number 40711396

Cheque 100106
Date: 24/04/X7
Payee: Harry Rumsden Wholesalers
£ 139.55

Cumbria Bank Plc — 40-70-68
High Street, Kendal
24/04 20 X7
Pay Harry Rumsden Wholesalers or order
one hundred and thirty nine pounds and 55p
£ 139.55
Easy-Grow Ltd
Cheque Number 100106 Branch number 40 7068 Account Number 40711396

TASK 2

RECONCILIATION OF LEDGER ACCOUNTS WITH SUPPLIES ACCOUNTS AS AT 31.3.X7

(a) **ANGLIAN TIMBER LTD**

	£
Balance as per purchase ledger	1,040.17
Add: returns not yet received by supplier	79.10
Balance as per supplier's statement	1,119.27

Solutions to trial run devolved assessments

(b) J CATON & CO

	£
Balance as per purchase ledger	-
Add: invoice not yet received by Grow-Easy Ltd	108.50
Balance as per suppliers' statement	108.50

TASK 3

Standing orders	Action
Northern Gas Board	The bank statement has a standing order charge which differs from the standing order details. I would check with the accountant and the bank, if necessary, to resolve the discrepancy. (£1,260.00 ÷ 12 = £105)

TASK 4

Petty cash voucher	Action
Postage: Claim No 1 for £7.40	Process
Postage: Claim No 2 for £4.90	There is no receipt to support this claim (only 3 receipts are included in the data none of which is for this claim) Ask the claimant to provide a receipt and do not process.
Stationery: £14.95	Exceeds authorisation limit, pass to the accountant for approval.
Taxi: £5.75	Process

TASK 5

Date 20X7	Postage £	Travel/taxis £	Stationery £	General £	Total £
17 April b/d - Receipt					(100.00)
18 April	2.40	6.90	-	2.00	11.30
19 April	4.90	14.10	6.75	11.45	37.20
20 April	1.20	-	2.25	1.05	4.50
21 April	-	-	2.90	-	2.90
22 April	1.10	1.25	0.90	-	3.25
23 April	2.40	1.15	2.00	1.00	6.55
24 April	7.40	5.75	-	-	13.15
Totals	19.40	29.15	14.80	15.50	78.85
24 April Balance c/d					21.15
					100.00
25 April Balance b/d					21.15
Bank					78.85
					100.00

Solutions to trial run devolved assessments

ASSESSMENT CRITERIA

Task 1

The six cheques must be completed neatly and accurately with no more than two errors allowed.

Task 2

The two ledger accounts must be completed accurately and reconciled to the suppliers accounts. One error allowed.

Task 3

The Gas Board standing order must be identified as an error.

Task 4

The postage claim for £4.90 and the stationery claim for £14.95 must be identified as needing corrective action.

Task 5

The petty cash book must be completed accurately and neatly.

Overall assessment

Students may be allowed to make further minor errors, provided they do not suggest a fundamental lack of understanding.

Students must not be penalised more than once for the same error. If a student transfers an incorrect figure to another part of the exercise, this is not counted as a further error.

SOLUTIONS TO TRIAL RUN DEVOLVED ASSESSMENT 4

WORKBASE OFFICE SUPPLIES

DO NOT TURN THIS PAGE UNTIL YOU HAVE
COMPLETED THE TRIAL RUN DEVOLVED ASSESSMENT

SOLUTIONS

TASK 1

A suitable invoice stamp might look like the one below.

```
┌─────────────────────────────────────────────┐
│  RECEIVED              DD Month YY          │
│  No: XXXX                                   │
├─────────────────────────────────────────────┤
│  Checked to Purchase Order No:   ☐☐☐☐      │
│                        Prices               │
│                    Quantities               │
│       Checked to GRN No:         ☐☐☐☐      │
│                    Quantities               │
│               In good condition             │
│  Supplier terms/discount agreed             │
│                VAT rate agreed              │
│  Calculations: Price extensions             │
│                     Additions               │
│                     Discount                │
│                          VAT                │
├─────────────────────────────────────────────┤
│  Exceptions  ..............................  │
│  Initials  ...............   Date  ........  │
│  Payment authorised  ......  Date  ........  │
└─────────────────────────────────────────────┘
```

TASK 2

WORKBASE OFFICE SUPPLIES LTD

MEMORANDUM

To: Mr Denton
From: A Technician
Re: *Purchase invoices 31/8/X5*

I have performed the usual checks on suppliers' invoices submitted to me today. Apart from the following problem invoices, I have passed the purchase invoices for your authorisation.

1   *Beacon Ltd Inv 117382*

   (a) The discount stated on our purchase order is 20%, but we have only been given 15% on the invoice. I intend to request a revised invoice or, alternatively, a credit note for the additional discount. Firstly, though, I will check with Mrs Tarvey that we are due 20%.

   (b) The GRN states that one of the filing cabinets was badly dented and was sent back to Beacon. I will request a credit note for this item.

2   *Ryemead Ltd Inv 9942*

   There is a mistake on the invoice: the quantity of slate blue filing trays is 5, but the total cost has been calculated for 10. I will ask for a credit note before allowing the invoice to go ahead for processing.

TASK 3

Item

				£	£

(i)   DEBIT   Purchase ledger - Kineton Ltd (021K)   82.00★
       CREDIT   Sales ledger - Kineton Ltd (K022)   82.00★
       DEBIT   Purchase ledger control   82.00
       CREDIT   Sales ledger control   82.00
       Being contra entry

(ii)   DEBIT   Purchase ledger - Beacon Ltd (042B)   39.44★
       CREDIT   Purchase ledger - Beacon Ltd (33B)   39.44★
       Being set-off between accounts of the same supplier

(iii)   DEBIT   Purchase ledger control (3000)   610.00
       CREDIT   Sales ledger control (2000)   610.00
       Being correction of incorrect posting of cash receipt

(iv)   CREDIT   Purchase ledger - Weston Supplies (041W)   18.00★
       Being correction of incorrect invoice amount posted to memorandum account

(v)   DEBIT   Sales ledger control (2000)   472.05
       CREDIT   Purchase ledger control (3000)   472.05
       Being correction of incorrect posting of supplier's invoice

★ These are entries to memorandum accounts.

Other items

Item (vi) does not require any journal entries to be made.

Item (vi) requires a correction of the total of purchase ledger balances.

ASSESSMENT CRITERIA

Task 1

Rubber stamp appropriately designed. At least 12 of the 16 items shown in our solution should be present in one form or another.

Task 2

Validation checks correctly carried out. Only one error/omission allowed.

Task 3

Journal entries must be correct. Only one error is allowed.

SOLUTIONS TO TRIAL RUN DEVOLVED ASSESSMENT 5

PAPER PRODUCTS

DO NOT TURN THIS PAGE UNTIL YOU HAVE
COMPLETED THE TRIAL RUN DEVOLVED ASSESSMENT

SOLUTION

TASK 1
PURCHASES DAY BOOK

Date	Details	Goods £	VAT £	Total £
8 May	Murray Bros	741.30	129.73	871.03
9 May	Johnson & Co	142.00	24.85	166.85
14 May	Drury & Brown	407.50	71.31	478.81
17 May	Lever Bros	86.30	15.10	101.40
18 May	Bell and Davies	107.58	18.83	126.41
20 May	Lancs CC	1,110.48	194.33	1,304.81
22 May	John Dawson	15.97	2.79	18.76
22 May	The Paper Shop	222.20	38.89	261.09
26 May	Sams Supplies	346.47	60.63	407.10
27 May	Speakman Products	115.99	20.30	136.29
		3,295.79	576.76	3,872.55

TASK 2
PURCHASE LEDGER

MURRAY BROS

	£			£
c/d	871.03	8 May	Purchases	871.03
			b/d	871.03

JOHNSON & CO

	£			£
c/d	166.85	9 May	Purchases	166.85
			b/d	166.85

DRURY & BROWN

	£			£
c/d	478.81	14 May	Purchases	478.81
			b/d	478.81

LEVER BROS

	£			£
c/d	101.40	17 May	Purchases	101.40
			b/d	101.40

BELL AND DAVIES

	£			£
c/d	126.41	18 May	Purchases	126.41
			b/d	126.41

5: Paper Products (solutions)

LANCS CC

	£			£
c/d	1,304.81	20 May	Purchases	1,304.81
			b/d	1,304.81

JOHN DAWSON

	£			£
c/d	18.76	22 May	Purchases	18.76
			b/d	18.76

THE PAPER SHOP

	£			£
c/d	261.09	22 May	Purchases	261.09
			b/d	261.09

SAMS SUPPLIES

	£			£
c/d	407.10	26 May	Purchases	407.10
			b/d	407.10

SPEAKMAN PRODUCTS

	£			£
c/d	136.29	27 May	Purchases	136.29
			b/d	136.29

TASKS 3 AND 4

MAIN (NOMINAL) LEDGER

PURCHASES ACCOUNT

		£		£
May 20X7	Total purchases	3,295.79		

VAT ACCOUNT

		£		£
May 20X7	VAT on purchases	576.76		

CREDITORS ACCOUNT

	£			£
		May 20X7	Purchases	3,872.55

Solutions to trial run devolved assessments

ASSESSMENT CRITERIA

Task 1

The purchases day book must be accurate and completed correctly. No more than one error allowed.

Tasks 2, 3 and 4

Details must be transferred accurately and neatly to the various accounts. All the relevant columns must be completed.

SOLUTIONS TO TRIAL RUN DEVOLVED ASSESSMENT 6

CATERING CONTRACTS

DO NOT TURN THIS PAGE UNTIL YOU HAVE COMPLETED THE TRIAL RUN DEVOLVED ASSESSMENT

SOLUTIONS

TASK 1

PURCHASES DAY BOOK

Date	Details	Goods £	VAT £	Total £
6 June	Thomas Hardy	74.80	13.09	87.89
7 June	Ealing & Co	176.95	30.97	207.92
11 June	Bryant Associates	243.44	42.60	286.04
14 June	Clark & Robinson	98.56	17.25	115.81
14 June	Bass Ltd	346.58	60.65	407.23
17 June	J Adams Ltd	106.00	18.55	124.55
21 June	W Larkin	37.59	6.58	44.17
23 June	J Bryers Ltd	179.56	31.42	210.98
24 June	A Stewart & Co	274.07	47.96	322.03
26 June	M Ealham Ltd	659.86	115.48	775.34
		2,197.41	384.55	2,581.96

TASK 2

PURCHASE LEDGER

THOMAS HARDY

		£			£
c/d		87.89	6 June	Purchases day book	87.89
			b/d		87.89

EALING & CO

		£			£
c/d		207.92	7 June	Purchases day book	207.92
			b/d		207.92

BRYANT ASSOCIATES

		£			£
c/d		286.04	11 June	Purchases day book	286.04
			b/d		286.04

CLARK & ROBINSON

		£			£
c/d		115.81	14 June	Purchases day book	115.81
			b/d		115.81

BASS LTD

		£			£
c/d		407.23	14 June	Purchases day book	407.23
			b/d		407.23

J ADAMS LTD

	£		£
c/d	124.55	17 June Purchases day book	124.55
		b/d	124.55

W LARKIN

	£		£
c/d	44.17	21 June Purchases day book	44.17
		b/d	44.17

J BRYERS LTD

	£		£
c/d	210.98	23 June Purchases day book	210.98
		b/d	210.98

A STEWART & CO

	£		£
c/d	322.03	24 June Purchases day book	322.03
		b/d	322.03

M EALHAM LTD

	£		£
c/d	775.34	26 June Purchases	775.34
		b/d	775.34

TASK 3

MAIN LEDGER

PURCHASES ACCOUNT

		£		£
June	Purchases	2,197.41	c/d	2,197.41
b/d		2,197.41		

VAT ACCOUNT

		£		£
June	VAT on purchases	384.55	c/d	384.55
b/d		384.55		

CREDITORS ACCOUNT

	£			£
c/d	2,581.96	June	Purchases	2,581.96
		b/d		2,581.96

TASK 4

Outstanding creditors at the end of June

Name	Amount
	£
Thomas Hardy	87.89
Ealing & Co	207.92
Bryant Associates	286.04
Clark & Robinson	115.81
Bass Ltd	407.23
J Adams Ltd	124.55
W Larkin	44.17
J Bryers Ltd	210.98
A Stewart & Co	322.03
M Ealham Ltd	775.34
Total	2,581.96

ASSESSMENT CRITERIA

Task 1

Figures must be correctly worked out for the purchases day book and transferred accurately into the day book. No more than one error is allowed.

Task 2

The invoice values must be transferred correctly to the purchase ledger. No more than one error allowed.

Task 3

The correct entries must be transferred to the purchases, VAT and creditors account. No more than one error is allowed.

Task 4

The list of outstanding creditors produced must be accurate and balance to the relevant figures in the ledger.

AAT – Unit 2 Making and Recording Payments DA Kit (8/00)

ORDER FORM

Any books from our AAT range can be ordered by telephoning 020-8740-2211. Alternatively, send this page to our address below, fax it to us on 020-8740-1184, or email us at **publishing@bpp.com**. Or look us up on our website: www.bpp.com

We aim to deliver to all UK addresses inside 5 working days; a signature will be required. Order to all EU addresses should be delivered within 6 working days. All other orders to overseas addresses should be delivered within 8 working days.

To: BPP Publishing Ltd, Aldine House, Aldine Place, London W12 8AW

Tel: 020-8740 2211   Fax: 020-8740 1184   Email: publishing@bpp.com

Mr / Ms (full name): _____

Daytime delivery address: _____

_____

Postcode: _____   Daytime Tel: _____

Please send me the following quantities of books.

	5/00 Interactive Text	8/00 DA Kit	8/00 CA Kit
FOUNDATION			
Unit 1 Recording Income and Receipts (7/00 Text)	☐	☐	
Unit 2 Making and Recording Payments (7/00 Text)	☐	☐	
Unit 3 Ledger Balances and Initial Trial Balance (7/00 Text)	☐	☐	
Unit 4 Supplying information for Management Control (6/00 Text)	☐		
Unit 20 Working with Information Technology (8/00 Text)	☐		
Unit 22/23 Achieving Personal Effectiveness (7/00 Text)	☐		
INTERMEDIATE			
Unit 5 Financial Records and Accounts	☐	☐	
Unit 6 Cost Information	☐	☐	
Unit 7 Reports and Returns	☐	☐	
Unit 21 Using Information Technology	☐		
Unit 22: see below			
TECHNICIAN			
Unit 8/9 Core Managing Costs and Allocating Resources	☐		☐
Unit 10 Core Managing Accounting Systems	☐	☐	☐
Unit 11 Option Financial Statements (Accounting Practice)	☐		
Unit 12 Option Financial Statements (Central Government)	☐		
Unit 15 Option Cash Management and Credit Control	☐	☐	
Unit 16 Option Evaluating Activities	☐	☐	
Unit 17 Option Implementing Auditing Procedures	☐	☐	
Unit 18 Option Business Tax FA00 (8/00 Text)	☐	☐	
Unit 19 Option Personal Tax FA00 (8/00 Text)	☐	☐	
TECHNICIAN 1999			
Unit 17 Option Business Tax Computations FA99 (8/99 Text & Kit)	☐	☐	
Unit 18 Option Personal Tax Computations FA99 (8/99 Text & Kit)	☐	☐	
TOTAL BOOKS	☐ +	☐ +	☐ = ☐

@ £9.95 each = £ ☐

Postage and packaging:
UK: £2.00 for each book to maximum of £10
Europe (inc ROI and Channel Islands): £4.00 for first book, £2.00 for each extra
Rest of the World: £20.00 for first book, £10 for each extra

P & P   £ ☐

➤ Unit 22 Maintaining a Healthy Workplace Interactive Text (postage free)   ☐ @ £3.95   £ ☐

GRAND TOTAL   £ ☐

I enclose a cheque for £ _____ (cheques to BPP Publishing Ltd) or charge to Mastercard/Visa/Switch

Card number ☐☐☐☐ ☐☐☐☐ ☐☐☐☐ ☐☐☐☐

Start date _____   Expiry date _____   Issue no. (Switch only) ____

Signature _____

AAT - Unit 2 Making and Recording Payments DA Kit (8/00)

REVIEW FORM & FREE PRIZE DRAW

All original review forms from the entire BPP range, completed with genuine comments, will be entered into one of two draws on 31 January 2001 and 31 July 2001. The names on the first four forms picked out on each occasion will be sent a cheque for £50.

Name: _____   Address: _____

How have you used this Devolved Assessment Kit?
(Tick one box only)

- [ ] Home study (book only)
- [ ] On a course: college _____
- [ ] With 'correspondence' package
- [ ] Other _____

Why did you decide to purchase this Devolved Assessment Kit? *(Tick one box only)*

- [ ] Have used BPP Texts in the past
- [ ] Recommendation by friend/colleague
- [ ] Recommendation by a lecturer at college
- [ ] Saw advertising
- [ ] Other _____

During the past six months do you recall seeing/receiving any of the following?
(Tick as many boxes as are relevant)

- [ ] Our advertisement in *Accounting Technician* magazine
- [ ] Our advertisement in *Pass*
- [ ] Our brochure with a letter through the post

Which (if any) aspects of our advertising do you find useful?
(Tick as many boxes as are relevant)

- [ ] Prices and publication dates of new editions
- [ ] Information on Interactive Text content
- [ ] Facility to order books off-the-page
- [ ] None of the above

Have you used the companion Interactive Text for this subject?   [ ] Yes   [ ] No

Your ratings, comments and suggestions would be appreciated on the following areas

	Very useful	Useful	Not useful
Introductory section (How to use this Devolved Assessment Kit etc)	[ ]	[ ]	[ ]
Practice Activities	[ ]	[ ]	[ ]
Practice Devolved Assessments	[ ]	[ ]	[ ]
Trial Run Devolved Assessments	[ ]	[ ]	[ ]
AAT Sample Simulation	[ ]	[ ]	[ ]
Content of Answers	[ ]	[ ]	[ ]
Layout of pages	[ ]	[ ]	[ ]
Structure of book and ease of use	[ ]	[ ]	[ ]

	Excellent	Good	Adequate	Poor
Overall opinion of this Kit	[ ]	[ ]	[ ]	[ ]

Do you intend to continue using BPP Assessment Kits/Interactive Texts/?   [ ] Yes   [ ] No

Please note any further comments and suggestions/errors on the reverse of this page.

Please return to: Nick Weller, BPP Publishing Ltd, FREEPOST, London, W12 8BR

AAT - Unit 2 Making and Recording Payments DA Kit (8/00)

REVIEW FORM & FREE PRIZE DRAW (continued)

Please note any further comments and suggestions/errors below

FREE PRIZE DRAW RULES

1. Closing date for 31 January 2001 draw is 31 December 2000. Closing date for 31 July 2001 draw is 30 June 2001.

2. Restricted to entries with UK and Eire addresses only. BPP employees, their families and business associates are excluded.

3. No purchase necessary. Entry forms are available upon request from BPP Publishing. No more than one entry per title, per person. Draw restricted to persons aged 16 and over.

4. Winners will be notified by post and receive their cheques not later than 6 weeks after the relevant draw date.

5. The decision of the promoter in all matters is final and binding. No correspondence will be entered into.